THE
CAROLINA HOUSEWIFE

by Sarah Rutledge

A Facsimile of the 1847 Edition,
With an Introduction and a Preliminary Checklist
of South Carolina Cookbooks Published before 1935
By Anna Wells Rutledge

UNIVERSITY OF SOUTH CAROLINA PRESS

Published in Columbia, South Carolina, by the
University of South Carolina Press

First printing, 1979, hardcover
Second printing, 1980, paperback
Third printing, 1987, paperback
Fourth printing, 1991, hardcover
Fifth printing, 1999, hardcover

Manufactured in the United States of America

ISBN 0-87249-383-0

CONTENTS

INTRODUCTION

"The Carolina Housewife by a Lady of Charleston" was published in 1847, followed by other editions, all anonymous. (For until about 1920-odd the name of a Charleston woman appeared in print but thrice—when born, when married and when buried—the legal necessities.) Of course "everyone" (everyone being her friends and relations) knew that the book had been compiled by Sarah Rutledge, daughter of Edward Rutledge, a signer of the Declaration of Independence, and his wife, Henrietta Middleton Rutledge, a sister of Arthur Middleton, another signer of the Declaration of Independence from South Carolina. Cousin Sally was born in Charleston in 1782 and died here in 1855. That was the year a small book by "The Ancient Lady"—"The Octogenarian Lady"—was published. Mrs. Poyas (1792–1877) described what old time cooking was ". . . long before Miss Sally Rutledge had favored us with that excellent volume 'The Carolina House-wife or Cookery Book,' which she published for charitable purposes." Miss Rutledge probably turned in her grave at this. She was buried in St. Philips Churchyard. One wonders if Cousin Sally gave the copy for the inscription to the cutter of her father's tomb stone: there EDWARD RUTLEDGE is thus capitalized while "the almighty" is in lower case. (This has distressed pious members of the family for generations—it has amused the irreverent.)

To go back to "The Carolina Housewife," the fifth edition came out in 1963 and seems to have reached "rare book" status very promptly. I spent a delightful summer when with Charlotte Walker and Helen Rudisill we tried out receipts in the *Housewife*. This brought back to me the Charleston I first remember, let's say from after the hurricane of 1911. It was a pleasant rather small town with the "feel" and the "air" of a city. The pace was leisurely—gentlemen walked home to dinner at about three o'clock. This hour is an eighteenth-century continuation, also tropical. A nap was taken after dinner, then they returned to the office for a brief stay.

There was still in Charleston a "hangover" of the eighteenth and nineteenth centuries—architecture of course but other angles too, as well as the way of life of our time then—rice planters and rice planting, the busy local Market (back of the beautiful Hall), seeing the "Mosquito Fleet" come in, hearing and knowing the shrimp men and vegetable women, and seeing the turkey buzzards, an important division of early sanitation. Once I saw many of those buzzards circling over a wooded area—there must have been a dead animal below; I don't remember if it was over Hell Hole Swamp or Four Hole Swamp. This last is now owned by the Audubon Society. How grateful we must be and how pleased would be the great naturalist John James Audubon and his two sons (who married daughters of the great naturalist and Lutheran minister in Charleston, the Rev. John Bachman).

Growing up in Charleston one became aware of architecture at an early age—good, bad, and indifferent buildings in all sections, seen from the streetcar, on the way to and from Magnolia Cemetery and the Market, or when walking to church or school or to Mr. Ohlandt's grocery.

I vaguely remember the great 1911 hurricane which took down so many of the banks in the rice fields that the cost of rebuilding was prohibitive. This was the death blow to the planters. A friend and contemporary tells me he remembers seeing his grandfather looking at this rice in shuck in dry fields, ready to go for threshing. The waters rose and the planter stood watching his life work go down the river; he did not change expression.

But Carolina rice was not forgotten; between World Wars I and II a woman who grew up on a Combahee plantation was housekeeping in London and asked at "the Stores" (the Army-Navy, of course) if they carried "the very best rice." The old man's reply was "I'm sorry, Madam, but Carolina rice is no longer exported." This was approximately thirty years after the "Carolina Rice Cook Book" was put out by the *Carolina Rice Kitchen Association.* The recipes were compiled by Mrs. Samuel G. Stoney. After the title page came a "Charade," sixteen lines of verse by Eliza Peronneau Mathewes, and overleaf was the charade's "answer," a lyrical paragraph on "RICE BIRDS."

Select the fattest birds, remove the entrails, bake them whole or split them up the back and broil. Permit no sacrilegious hand to remove the head, for the base of the brain of the rice bird is the most succulent portion. Or the birds may be placed in either shape in a round bottom pot with a small lump of butter, pepper and salt, and cook over a quick fire. Use no fork in eating. Take the neck of the bird in the left hand and his little right leg in the right hand. Tear away the right leg and eat all but the extreme end of the bone. Hold the bill of the bird in one hand and crush your teeth through the back of the head, and thank Providence that you are permitted to live. Take the remaining left leg in your right hand and place in your mouth the entire body of the bird, and then munch the sweetest morsel that ever brought gustatory delight. All that remains is the front portion of the head and the tiny bits of bone that formed the ends of the legs. To leave more is to betray your unappreciativeness of the gift of the gods.

The bird referred to here is the bobolink or reed bird, the *Dolichonyx orryzivorus* of Linnaeus.

Market-going doesn't seem to have been a habit in Charleston (as it was in Savannah, Richmond, and Baltimore). The shrimp man, the vegetable woman, and the butcher were standbys. The "Shrimpy-raw-raw" call—each cook would recognize the distinct cry of her particular favorite—was a magnet for a kitchen exodus and then gossip on the curb. An account of these cries, *Street Cries of an Old Southern City* was printed by Harriette Kershaw Leiding in 1910. Sometime ago, at the time of one of the Azalea Festivals, the National Council of Teachers of English made Victrola records of these calls—would that they could now be put on tape. The vegetable carts came into the backyard—in our case it was that of "Old Emma" and the young 'uns. Both shrimp and vegetables were measured by the plate and with both one was given Broadus, which New Orleans calls *lagniappe*.

The Market stalls were stacked with produce; from the islands, from "Hungry Neck" (the Mount Pleasant area), from the rivers, parishes, and sea islands, boats came stacked with vegetables and these stacked with people; wagons came down loaded with stuff from "up the road." General Charles Cotesworth Pinckney (1746–1825) remembered that, aged seven, he saw the first wagon arriving in Charleston from the interior in 1753 and his father, Chief Justice Charles Pinckney, (c. 1699–1758) saying to his young son, "By the time you are a man, there will be at least twenty wagons coming to town." In later life Charles Cotesworth Pinckney would repeat this when he saw long lines arriving with materials for exporting and produce for the city. They must have seen many of the "King's trees" go out; today I had "a flashback" as a container truck (without the freezing unit) went down the State Road (the Broad Path) with seven tremendously tall pine trunks on it. By the first quarter of the twentieth century they were no longer coming as plentifully as they had before. Some of the wagons were tidy, some were untidy, with wobbly wheels and swaybacked horses or mules drawing them, but they were picturesque, as were the vegetable women who carried their loads in large round fanner baskets on their heads (fanner is a *Spartina* marsh grass bound with strips cut from the fronds of tall palmetto trees). The posture of these women was superb. Few of them sold flowers then, though that's what their modern successors do. Most retailers and vegetable women must have purchased their green groceries at the Market. Ohlandt's, Welch & Eason's, and Hurkamp's wagons and horses had such nice drivers, and "Old Emma's" cart was a wooden, wonderful, handle-pushed box on two noisy wheels.

The fishing fleet went over the bar in the earliest light and came back in at sunset—it was called *The Mosquito Fleet.* They looked like mosquitos—their coming into harbor on the southeast breeze, wing and wing, jib and mainsail out, men cleaning the fish and sea gulls following, screaming, was beautiful. Trawling has made this fleet almost a thing of the past, but one may still see something like it at Spikestown, Barbados. The boats and storms and fishing people of Dubose Heyward's (1885–1940) "Porgy" are authentic. (One little boat was named *The Too Sweet My Love.*)

Another food from the sea was the sea turtle, to be distinguished from the terrapins which are terrestrial and which we called *cooter* and also ate. "Old Mr. Magwood," at Mount Pleasant and "all over the place," had cooter pens; he and others up and down the coast supplied turtles to restaurants and hotels in Baltimore. They were delicious, as were sea turtle eggs whose shells were soft and pliable—shells children loved to punch. Children also enjoyed the digging up of the sea turtles' eggs in the sand dunes. A cooter nest might be noted in a soft, shady spot exposed to both morning and evening sun for hatching warmth. The hole was made by the cooter pushing one back foot into the sandy spot and circling to make a hole in which to deposit the eggs.

When there was a turtle in the tin tub in the basement, its decapitation was a social event, for it was difficult to catch the head out of its shell. At the pineland house there was always a cooter barrel by the well; when it got overcrowded, stew was made. At *Middleburg* on the Eastern Branch of the Cooper River, Maum Phyllis Coasum was famous for her cooter soup and always wanted cooter eggs for hers.

Maum Phyllis also used eggs—hen's unlaid ones—in stuffing for fowl. There was a plantation saying "Thunder do roll—turtle do walk." If one was bitten or clawed by a cooter, common knowledge (or superstition) felt it would not let loose 'till thunder. At plantations too were oyster barrels. When oyster stew came you knew they had reached the state they *had* to be cooked!

Around the beginning of World War I, we used to swim from the dairy wharf off the Boulevard and a great sea turtle used to watch us regularly with interest.

As against turtles and cooters, shark has always been a matter of taste; some like it, many won't eat it (does plugged shark meat frequently pass as scallops now?). Once, some days after a Fourth of July picnic, I was rowed across to Kiawah Island and walked across the picnic ground. There had been a large fire and many shark fins, charred and uncharred, were still piled around it; on top of the pile was a pair of high-heeled black satin slippers. ("Conjer" Voodoo? Remember the scene in *Porgy and Bess?*)

Then the Battery Dairy and their boat coming over at about six o'clock from Mr. Lawton's place on James Island. The loud cheerful banging of milk tins by the docking hands was followed by the horses and wagons going out with the bottles, while a social situation developed with nearby nurses, waitresses, and children coming to the dairy for milk (our piazza commanded a view up the long alley). Some families had a cow, which went up to the North Carolina mountains with them in the summer and came back in the fall. And the seasonal things like the wall-to-wall carpets and matting for winter and summer come back to mind.

All the daily happenings and routines, like counting the flat silver each evening and taking all silver upstairs (I know one household—the head of it well on the way to being a centenarian—who did this in the 1950s). Then the lady of the house, or housekeeper, each day with her key basket, giving out supplies from the locked store room door—this done well into the twentieth century—the rice and grist from 100-pound barrels.

Of course daily there were *dahs*, nurses or nannies visiting in the yard with their children in "Charleston sunbonnets." "Dah" in some African language means father or mother. At Eutaw in the 1840s and '50s some of their old Africans taught children to count in their language—and some words, "these young," when really old, wondered if they *were* what they had been told. These dahs joined each other with

the carriages and go-carts (a "goe-cart" was in an inventory of a cler-
gyman in 1744) going to the nearest park—the Battery, City Hall Park
(really Washington Park), Colonial Lake (long less formally called Rutledge Street Pond), and the Dueling Grounds, Race Track, or the Exposition grounds—overlapping open land—now Hampton Park, and
The Citadel area—and the High Battery was to be gone on only with
a grown-up. And when and who had gone and was going to *The* Mountains, to Sewanee or to *The* Island. And joggling boards!

Then the Ice Wagon and Mr. Heron, the driver of the handsome
heavy horses—they had to be heavy to pull the great blocks of ice; ice
was sold by the hundred pounds and big tongs were carried by power-
ful men who rather disdained persons who took less than 75 pounds—
some people took 150 pounds. The men stood and walked with their
inside arms in the opposite shoulder, the outside arms holding handles
of tongs—this counterbalancing, bracing off and "giving a push" as it
was said. On very hot days Mr. Heron would spoil us with "snow balls,"
shaved ice made into balls and put in saucers.

Then there were the fire engine horses; once our piazza was being
scraped down for repainting, one night a post was smoldering and an
engine with the horses and bells and hose and firemen came down; we
went to the window in our nightdrawers to watch.

In February was the George Washington's Birthday parade with a
company of cavalry from Fort Moultrie (once a horse reared in front of
us). Next to the last section in the parade were the Porter Military
Academy boys, behind them came the Jenkins Orphanage Band. It was
difficult to tell when the Jenkins Orphanage Band started or ended as
their retinue of dancing and singing boys went along too (remember
this in the opera *Porgy and Bess*?).

And then the last doctor with his coach dog under his buggy (under
a coach is where a Dalmatian belongs), and then the last carriage and
pair and the last Victoria. Then the dory races and Porgy and his goat,
the Clyde Line steamers, the chimney sweeps ("ro-ro boys"), light-
wood sellers, the lamplighters, gaslight globes and mantles in the house,
lots of cobblestone streets, red flags going up as storm warnings and
the bells ringing at two o'clock to warn one of a freeze—to fill tubs and
cut off water—and of course Mr. Ladaveze and his wonderful candy
and the only girl with a pony, who rode with her father and grandfather
early each morning.

But let's return to the eighteenth and the mid-nineteenth centuries
with our author.

Although "a lady" had no biography, a certain amount has been "dug out" about her. Sally Rutledge stayed in England with Mr. and Mrs. Thomas Pinckney when Pinckney was minister to the Court of St. James. Thomas Pinckney was her father's partner-at-law; Sally was then around ten years old. Her father wrote to her saying that he was glad she was "learning music and dancing . . . they were pleasing accomplishments." He wrote too that her present of handkerchiefs (English "kerchiefs" for the head) sent to her maid Pansy, had been received, and that Pansy sent "sincere thanks and love"; Pansy had also received "with great delight your present of the ear-rings; and I assure you she has made the most of them; for she dressed herself out in them in five minutes after she got them and has never made her appearance without them since she first put them into her ears. Your Mama tells her she believes she sleeps in them but she won't admit it, tho we believe it. However, she came and told your Mother with great delight, a few days ago, that she had been offered four & then five guineas for them but that nothing should tempt her to part with them."

Miss Rutledge resided and probably tried out her recipes in various kitchens over many years—first in the family house at the corner of Broad and Orange streets; probably by 1802 at her stepmother's (who in the Directory for that year was listed as "Rutledge, Mary, lady of the late Governor obit . . . ") or at her brother's (Henry Middleton Rutledge) on Front Street at Federal Green. In 1806 and 1807 she is listed at No. 22, Church Street; in 1809 she was "Rutledge, Sarah, planter, Corner St. Philips and Boundary Streets"; the Directory of 1816 listed her at No. 17, St. Philips Street. For some years between 1813 and 1822 Mrs. Edward Rutledge, widow, lived on Tradd Street and, after 1829 and into the 1830s, on the northwest corner of Lamboll and Legaré streets. There can be little doubt that her stepdaughter was living with her. When Mrs. Rutledge died in 1839, Sarah was residuary legatee and executrix, with a legacy of five hundred dollars.

The will of Governor Edward Rutledge (1749–1800) among other things requested that his wife " . . . be supplied from the Plantations which are the joint property of General Pinckney and myself, with such things as are convenient and commonly furnished to our houses from thence, so long as the property shall be undivided, and this part of my Will, I confide particularly to the care of my dear friend Pinckney. . . ."

Edward Rutledge and Charles Cotesworth Pinckney (1745/6–1825) were brothers-in-law, each as his first wife having married a daughter of Henry Middleton (1717–1784) of Middleton Place, Ashley River.

Charles Cotesworth Pinckney outlived his brother-in-law by twenty-five years. His will, made in 1807 and proved in 1825, by codicil of 1824 left his late wife's niece, Sarah Rutledge, seven thousand dollars in 6 percent stock of the United States. Evidently there was intimacy as well as relationship, for by 1849 Miss Sarah Rutledge was living with her first cousin, Miss Harriott Pinckney (1776–1866), the last of the daughters of Charles Cotesworth Pinckney, at the very handsome Pinckney residence on East Bay, above Market Street at Guignard Street. This was burned in the fire of 1861. Miss Pinckney in 1853 laid off a corner of her yard, 140 feet on Market Street by 95 feet on East Bay, to be held in trust for profit until such time that funds should accrue from rental sufficient to finance the erection of a church for the use of seamen in the port. The Protestant Episcopal Church and the Rev. Mr. Charles Cotesworth Pinckney (1812–1898) were trustees in 1877. In 1916, The Church of the Redeemer was built as a Seaman's Bethel, with an adjunct called the Harriott Pinckney Home.

And now to cooking—but transportation and localities should come together first.

Tide, time, rivers high or low, timber, transportation, Broad Path, tracks, trucks, ferries, bridges, and defense often equaled places, food, communication. The time of early Huguenot church services varied as the tide affected their coming into town from French Quarter Creek on the Eastern Branch of the Cooper River. They came by canoes, oars, sail, steam—people, pitch, provisions, and rice.

By 1842 a packet boat made a 5 A.M. start up Cooper River, went as far as *Fairlawn* and was back at night. Near town were fields and meadows, then valuable estates, acres of swamps of first quality, larger or smaller "gangs of operators" (Dr. Irving's expression), and an unbroken sea of cultivated rice fields. There was association in the steamboat with passengers getting on and off at stated stops. Many from St. Thomas Parish descended at the *Brick Yard* plantation. The conversation was politics and planting. Cooper River people *were* rice. As were the planters on the Combahee, and those on the five great rivers of Georgetown. These were the North Santee and the South Santee, the Sampit, the Black, the Little Pee Dee and the Great Pee Dee, the Waccamaw and, at the end, Winyah Bay.

Everything and everyone alike and different: the land, the inhabitants and the crops. The Ashley River was again another picture—small fields, high yield and seed rice—with the planters in the neighborhood having the English county family feeling and outlook. I don't think a steamboat had a regular run up the Ashley, while Georgetown shipped to Charleston after the regular steamboat trips started.

All angles of the Georgetown planters, planting, and plantations may be read of in George Roger's *History* of the county (1970) while that of Cooper River may be followed through Dr. John B. Irving's "Day on Cooper River" (1842). Generations, time and change, timber, rice, brick, tiles, and marl to the Navy Yard, the Port Terminal, and the Santee-Cooper and Lake Marion.

Before 1861–65 and naval warfare along the South Carolina coast, particularly from Beaufort and St. Helena through Charleston, there had been steamboat transportation and sport fishing (as the expression goes today).

From the 1880s to around 1916 the only transportation to and from some islands between Beaufort and Charleston was by the boats successively named *The Pilot Boy*, *The New Pilot Boy*, *The Marion*, and *The Islander*. Landing at Accommodation and Union Wharfs, Charleston, they brought in Irish potatoes, cabbages, and cotton. Sea Island cotton was in long and rather narrow bales, square bales for the other. The boats had an upper and lower deck. Ten state rooms with two beds in each were off the upper deck. On the lower deck were food, fowl, freight, and figures. In the eighteenth century the gazettes listed arrivals with some notes on loads, names of persons of standing on board and the number of "deck passengers." Though not listed as such in the papers in the twentieth century the accommodation was the same, also in the Caribbean (I saw such in the 1940s).

The three owners of *The Marion* and *The Islander* were of Charleston. Two of them, the purser and the engineer, married Beaufort ladies and lived in Beaufort. The third, the captain, never married and kept on living in Charleston. Josh, the fireman, lived in Beaufort. The boat left Beaufort regularly once a week, the time depending on the tide—the depth of the water in the shallow places—but during the vegetable season the boat left Beaufort as soon as it was loaded and unloaded to get back to Charleston. It went to Savannah only when it got an order.

From Beaufort there were annual excursions on the boat—the Negroes' picnic on Decoration Day and the Baptist Church's picnic to Bluffton. Parents rowed their children from Hilton Head to Bluffton for it. The boat took general freight, food, lots of Sea Island cotton bales, and sometimes phosphate from the 1880s through 1915. It always stopped at Edisto Island at the public landing. On Wadmalaw there was Seabrook's Landing with the house up on a hill, the public landing at Martin's Point and, perhaps, landing at New Cut. On Yonges Island there was the public landing. The Johns Island bridge over the Stono opened for the boat.

Sea Islanders loved the coming of the boat. On Edisto a boy hearing the whistle would run to meet the boat—to look at the engine and talk to the engineer, a great reader with many books. From Wadmalaw they said the boat was their only way of getting to Charleston. At Dale on St. Helena Island there was a cotton gin. The workmen sang as they loaded the boat with long bales of beautiful Sea Island cotton, just as the workmen sang as they worked in the cotton fields in "Red Hills."

Small launches bought or made by islanders ran the steamboats out of business, circa 1914. Then improved roads and automobiles and trucks and other bridges made the business a loser.

At a Fripp plantation near Ocatee River and Creek in Jasper County, the owner sold to a Hunting Club, becoming their supervisor (and host) in 1916. He continued to grow sugarcane and yellow corn, which was ground into yellow grist; they roasted coffee in their ovens and ground it; they made delicious cane syrup, yellow hominy, and freshly roasted coffee for breakfast for their school teacher/boarder, with later homemade butter and fish caught and cooked during school hours by the wife, who said her recreation was fishing.

Well over one hundred and five years before the *Carolina Housewife* appeared, cookbooks were known in South Carolina—manuscript ones, of course, such as those kept by Eliza Lucas Pinckney (1720–1793). In an inventory of 1741 (that of Thomas Gadsden) were listed a *Book of Receipts* by Hannah Westy, and the *Art of Candying and Preserving Fruits and Flowers*, *A Table of Bees*, *The Dutch Gardener* by Henry Vanosten, and "320 Civil Oranges which grow'd in the garden." I am indebted to Walter Edgar for notes from his doctoral dissertation on Libraries of Colonial South Carolina.

Inventories give other titles and list contents of the houses, of course—furniture and the silver and china (now called by that awful phrase "a place setting"). As fascinating as all was the kitchen furniture, often with water plates showing that there was some distance from the dining room to the kitchen, down to "an Indian pott," a "Raisin jarr." There were in the inventories parcels of rice, barrels of rice, parcels of corn, and parcels of corn in the ear.

As well as with the uses of Indian corn, the first families of America are credited by Miss Rutledge with one recipe, that for Seminole Soup:

"Take a squirrel, cut it up and put it on to boil. When the soup is nearly done add to it one pint of picked hickory-nuts and a spoonful of parched and powdered sassafras leaves—or the tender top of a pine tree, which gives a very aromatic flavor to the soup."

The *Carolina Rice Cookbook* gives "An Indian Pilau," credit going to *The Maryland Kitchen*.

Beyond corn we are obliged to the Indians for knowledge of shellfish roasted; oysters were offered to the Spaniards at Port Royal in 1566. Almost a hundred and fifty years later Lawson saw Indians preferring bobcat over turkey. The Indians probably also ate possum. Certainly possum pie has been a staple delicacy in some country areas and with hunters.

The Indians had no known fermented drink, yet in the late nineteenth and early twentieth centuries a person whose taste and manner were old-fashioned brewed wines from native plants—blackberry wine, scuppernong wine, elderberry wine, muscadine wine, dandelion wine, persimmon and locust beer.

Miss Rutledge does not mention the great flocks of passenger pigeons (*Ectopistes migratorius*), but she must have seen or heard of them; there were still great clouds of them in the 1870s in upper South Carolina. Her two recipes for pigeons are very French, one a ragout. Both would be good for squab, the largest nursery producing them today being "The Palmetto Pigeon Plant" near Sumter, South Carolina. Unfortunately this was not of her time. Recently Wendell Levy (1891–1976), one of the owner-operators of this plant gave his extraordinary library in that field and his great collection of books on the *Camellia japonica* to the College of Charleston, of which he was a graduate.

The first decade in the new land, settled circa 1670–1680, must have been grim, to say the least. By 1682 Thomas Amy (not Thomas Ash, to whom the account is usually credited) recorded that " . . . now their Gardens begin to be supplied with such European plants and Herbs as are necessary for the Kitchen. . . ." He also noted the Indian use of corn when parched and powdered, saying it "was a Grain of General Use to Man and Beast, . . . " adding that in Carolina the settlers "have lately invented a way of making with it good sound Beer; but it's strong and heady. By maceration, when duly fermented, a strong spirit like Brandy may be drawn off from it, by the help of an Alembick." Could this be a prelude to the corn whiskey made in stills (illegally) all over Carolina and bought in "Prohibition Times" by persons who would have scorned it before? (I am indebted to Dr. St. Julien

Childs and to Gene Waddell, Director of the South Carolina Historical Society, for this note.)

Hardships persisted, and Judith Manigault (d. 1711), the wife of Peter Manigault (d. 1729), the Huguenot immigrant, wrote that "After our arrival in Carolina, we suffered every kind of evil. In about eighteen months our elder brother, unaccustomed to the hard labor we were obliged to undergo, died of a fever. Since leaving France we had experienced every kind of affliction—disease, pestilence, famine, poverty, hard labor. I have been for six months together without tasting bread, working the ground like a slave; and I have even passed three of four years without always having it when I wanted it. God has done great things for us in enabling us to bear up under so many trials." They had come to Carolina in 1685.

When the naturalist Mark Catesby set out into the woods up the rivers, into the Piedmont and the mountains in the 1720s (with Indians as guides and bearers) he said "to the Hospitality and Assistance of these friendly *Indians* I am much indebted, for I not only subsisted on what they shot but . . . " that to protect him and his paper, paints and specimens, they erected a bark hut "to keep me and my cargo from wet."

Nicholas de Longuemere, the Huguenot goldsmith and silk dealer, also carried other things. His 1703–1711 Account Book is in French, English, and a melange of both. In 1707 he recorded "un grand demy quartrier de derriere d'un grand beuf," "un quarter de vache," "27 lb. viande;" *rum* is "Rome," "Rhome," "Rom."

Lawson (*c.* 1701) stopped with the French on the Santee River, saying that in Carolina there were "no strict laws to bind our privileges. A Quest after Game, being as freely and peremptorily enjoyed by the meanest Planter Settler as he that is the highest in Dignity, or wealthiest in the Province. . . . A poor Labourer, that is Master of his Gun, hath as good a Claim to have continued courses of Delicacies crowded upon his Table, as he that is Master of a greater Purse." Later Lawson was burned at the stake by Indians in North Carolina.

Contemporary accounts of how the people lived beyond the overwritten Charleston area and the rice plantations are hard to find in print, or have not been put into print. We may follow Catesby and "T. A., Gent" with others who were good enough to leave records. For years I've had a "Berkeley Square" feeling about "this our Land."

The interlocking, expanding world of the eighteenth century on this new continent and in this new land may be observed through contemporary accounts in a small section of upstate South Carolina, with commercial, political, agricultural, and intellectual points. In the 1760s the clays of the neighborhood were of interest to the Wedgewoods, and young Thomas Griffiths was sent out to investigate exportation. He set out from Charleston to go towards the Cherokee Nation. After days of hard travel, near Cuffytown Creek, he " . . . bot some corn for my horse and potato bread and a fowl which I briled under a pine tree. . . . I saw a hunter hawling in a Wild Turkey Cock that weighed 26 lb. when drawd."

Almost twenty years after Griffiths, in the 1780s in that neighborhood at a plantation once called *Hard Labor* but when owned by Andrew Williamson called *White Hall*, a party of British officers was entertained, this after the fall of Charleston. Williamson, once with "patriots," had changed sides, this unknown to a neighbor who rode over for a "social day." This guest, an American, wrote that he afterwards said to Williamson that when " . . . the cloth was removed and wine introduced, you requested your guests to fill their glasses, and to my utter confusion gave as the first toast 'The King!' Well, I had no personal quarrel with King George (so I satisfied my honor) and drank it, but in that glass I drank farewell to all further intercourse with Gen. Williamson."

In the 1820s, '30s, and '40s and later at *Oakwood* in the Abbeville, McCormick, Greenwood area, was Mary Moragné, granddaughter of one of the 1764 Huguenots reaching South Carolina by mistake and settling in the Long Cane Creek–Little River Neighborhood, about three miles from the Savannah River. There they made a "planned town" called New Bordeaux, wishing to go into planting grapes for wine and to grow silk and flax—these and the climate defeated them. Cotton and corn were the successors.

Twenty years old, Mary Moragné, *circa* 70 years after 1764, was enjoying French eighteenth-century classics and "The American way of life" (or was it the South Carolina way of life?). In 1839 she wrote of a Fourth of July barbecue " . . . the family went in two carriage loads. This 'cue like all other 'cues consisted in eating a great deal and having a great deal more than could be eaten—although there were a great many persons present. . . . these ceremonies over, we all partook standing of a dinner in the grove . . . the gentlemen of our party took us to the carriage & treated us to as many fine watermellons as we could eat, brought from Augusta." (These Fourth of July barbecues continue to be held there to this day.)

In the neighborhood of the barbecue, the "social day," the "dinner briled under a pine tree," two names are applied to sections. One, *The Nation*, goes back to the purchase of land from the Cherokee Nation around 1761; no reasons seem known for what is now called "The Dark Corner." From the mid-eighteenth century to today it has been a place inhabited by persons of taste and knowledge, students, authors, scholars.

In *Red Hills and Cotton*, Ben Robertson (1903–1943) enlightened the world about the time lag (to use the present phrase) in his Valley— Twelve Mile. The quantity of food was all from their land, great quantities of land. Both are given a quantity of pages, as are his "kin" on Pea Ridge between Glassy and Six Mile mountains, with others to the west on the banks of the Keowee River. His grandmother, strong, tranquil, serene, would face life with equanimity—all but hawks after her chickens. Then "she would grab a shotgun. She shot at many hawks in her lifetime, she killed quite a few."

In the same period was Harry Legaré Watson's (1876–1956) edition of the *Index-Journal* in Greenwood. He knew his county and periods and made sure that the inhabitants didn't forget, as does his daughter Margaret Watson in "Greenwood County Sketches: Old Roads and Early Families." So, too, does their acquaintance, friend and neighbor, Louis B. Wright, whose *Barefoot in Arcadia* gave, he said, " . . . some aspects of life in a small town on the edge of the country in upper South Carolina during the first two decades of the twentieth century."

He remembers the sons of a tenant farmer "who knew all the lore of frontiersmen," saw where possums and turtles had walked, saw bee trees, knew every edible weed and root, as well as those good for poultices and herb tea. He tells us not only of the life but of the good food prepared by Flora who "never read a recipe but who would have made Julia Child pale into insignificance."

Our other contemporary from around there is Dr. Julian Boyd who knows more of Thomas Jefferson's tastes in food and drink than others, yet the first item in his bibliographical record is "Hog and Hominy: A Gastronomic Interpretation of Southern History."

Let us go back some years before the Revolution and then just before it. The seventeenth-century note of Amy's shows taste and flavor. Less than a hundred years later there are other opinions.

Charles Woodmason had been in South Carolina for about a dozen years before going back to England and being ordained. In 1763, on his return, he took, as itinerant minister, the new parish of St. Marks, cut out in 1757 on the northwest line of Williamsburg to the Pee Dee and Santee rivers, and his Journal in the 1760s gives you a picture of the difficulties on a raw frontier and its very hard life. He could seldom get necessities from the coast as the wagons going up and down were seasonal, meat and fish scarce, and after a great drought "the Mills Stand still having no Water to grind." They were reduced to boiling apples and peaches and greens from the trees.

He also noted on the trip up and down the country in the late summer of 1768, at Camden: "Now will come on their season of Festivity and Drunkenness. The Stills will be soon at Work for to make Whiskey and Peach Brandy—in this Article, both Presbyterians and Episcopals very charitably agree (Viz) That of getting Drunk."

At about the same time, on the coast, " . . . the manner of living nearly the same as England . . . where rum is cheap the use of it will not be uncommon among the poorer classes of people but the gentlemen in general are sober, industrious and temperate. . . ." In the decade before, Dr. Milligan-Johnston listed punch, madeira, claret, port, and other wines, remarking that "the ladies, I mention it to their credit, are extremely temperate, and generally drink water."

Then came "the troubles"—in 1775 William Henry Drayton and others went on a mission to the Dutch settlers in the Congaree area, urging them to sign the "Association." This involved hard riding and speaking after Divine services; it met with little success. Drayton once concluded: " . . . finished the day with a barbequed beef."

Three months later, in November of 1775, Thomas Pinckney of the First South Carolina Regiment rode up from Charleston to the Camden neighborhood, recruiting. At one house, the woman denied keeping a tavern but they "saw a fine forequarter of venison Smoking in the Fire and some noble potatoes in the ashes." At Colonel Richardson's "Big Home" Plantation near Halfway Swamp they had a "hearty welcome . . . good beef, mutton, such nice Peach Pyes and cream and delicate syllabubs."

In the 1780s, before the close of the struggle, Francisco de Mirada, an international liberal, coming into South Carolina from South America via Cuba, described rice bread; he called it tortillas and he met it in Beaufort, North Carolina, and then in Georgetown; he wrote they were "excellent and it is also very healthful." (The *Carolina Housewife* gives thirty-six recipes for rice breads.)

After the struggle, at the end of April 1791 (?), President George Washington entered South Carolina. He was lavishly entertained both publicly and privately—once eighteen at breakfast. Often he advised the next house to receive him as to his probable time of arrival; he once added a postscript, "For God's sake give my rider some grog." On the way he noted riding twenty to thirty miles between meals or before breakfast. There were great public dinners in Charleston, Camden, and Columbia, where it was held in the State House, a "large and commodious building" but unfinished.

Advancing in time by about fifteen years we come to 1806 with Edward Hooker from New Haven who had just graduated from Yale, coming down to Charleston and riding up to Columbia, where his brother was practicing law. He stayed south for some time teaching, and set out with his friend, the Reverend Mr. Lilly, for a tour of seventeen days in the Carolina Mountains. Near the Woolenoy River they visited the house of a mountain preacher and thus described it:

> The house is a framed one—but has one story—comfortable size— furnished in a way and inhabited by a family exactly corresponding to the stile of the people, whose minister it belongs to. Our dinner . . . consisted of fresh pork and sweet potatoes cut up and set in a large tin pan, without any bread or sauce, or any accompaniment, except salt. A chest not higher than our knees served for a table:— The end of another chest served for a seat for our kind host; while my fellow traveller and myself occupied the only chairs in the room. . . . I have rarely, perhaps never, made a meal with more satisfaction. After prayers, we retired early to a coarse but comfortable bed, which was furnished with curtains of a coarse sort of gause. . . . Oct. 1, 1806. I came home (to Cambridge) in excellent health and with a fine stock of good spirits—and I brought with me some corrected notions of the Mountain people, who have not unfrequently been represented as intolerably savage in their manners.

Captain and Mrs. Basil Hall in 1827 and 1828 traveled down from Canada to New Orleans. Mrs. Hall's letters to her family were published a hundred years later as "The Aristocratic Journey." They went to a dinner in Columbia, South Carolina, where the company was "all gentlemen with the exception of four ladies belonging to the house." She thus described the edibles:

> . . . we went at half past four, and I must say that in spite of all my experience of the strange arrangements of American dinners I confess this style did astonish me, and what any of you who have never seen such would have thought I cannot say. There was a huge

party invited to meet us, all gentlemen with the exception of four ladies belonging to the house. I ought to premise that I had before been informed that both Mr. and Mrs. Taylor belonged to the old stock families in South Carolina, families who pique themselves on their ancient standing, quite the old aristocracy, in short, and possessing immense wealth. There was the same fuss before dinner of calling the mistress of the house out of the room and so on, and finally she and another elderly, female relation disappeared altogether and we found them standing ready placed at the upper end of the table, and then with one consent the gentlemen fell to carving the dishes nearest to them with a degree of dispatch and eagerness that I never saw equalled anywhere out of a steamboat. The top dish was a ham which Mrs. Taylor herself showed her power of carving upon by beginning to cut it in pieces from the knuckle upwards. The rest of the entertainment consisted of turkeys, roast and boiled, chickens, roast ducks, corned beef, and fish, together with various dishes of sweet potatoes, Irish potatoes, cabbage, rice, and beetroot, to demolish which we were furnished with two pronged forks, and if you were troublesome enough to call for a second knife you were furnished with one merely half wiped. For second course we had *eight pies* down the side of the table, six dishes of glasses of syllabub and as many of jelly, besides one or two "floating islands," as they denominate what we called whipped cream, and odd corners filled up by ginger and other preserves. I was fortunately well placed next an exceedingly agreeable old man, Judge De Saussure, a most gentlemanlike person. On the other side I had one of the young ladies of the house, for ladies in America have a vile custom of crowding all together at dinner tables and leave the gentlemen likewise to herd by themselves.

In August 1826 eighteen gentlemen went on a frolic (picnic) on the schooner *Margaret*. The claret, port, wine, and brandy—thirty-seven bottles in all—cost about $35.00, an average of about $2.00 each. The dinner for eighteen, including the ice was $20.25.

The next year Robert Gilmor, Jr. (1774–1848) of Baltimore visited James H. Ladson (1795–1868) in Charleston and on March 2 they went to the Jockey Club Ball. "The tables were set in the lower rooms and were profusely covered with every delicacy and champagne and madeira in great plenty. After the ladies retired, the gentlemen sat down and were furnished with excellent *beef steaks*, according to the custom here, but not usual elsewhere on similar occasions." Could this be a souvenir of the local eighteenth-century Beefsteak Club?

He remarked on the excellent wine at Mr. John Julius Pringle's (1753–1843) and said he and Mr. Van Buren had bought largely at an auction of John Middleton's wine (this must have been the John Middleton of Crowfield, 1784–1826). Two days after the Jockey Club Ball he went to Mr. John Gadsden's where the dinner was "turtle, venison, ham and turkey, and many other good dishes, with peas and asparagus. The conversation throughout the day was spirited. . . ."

In 1851 Mrs. Charles Alston gave a ball that one guest described as "the handsomest ever given in Charleston." Mrs. Alston's list of supplies reads as follows:

18 dozn plates—14 dozn knives—28 dozn spoons—6 dozn Wine-glasses—As many Chapaigne [*sic*] glasses as could be collected—4 wild Turkeys—4 hams 2 for sandwiches & 2 for the supper tables, 8 patés—60 partridges—6 pr of Pheasants—6 pr Canvassback Ducks—5 pr of our wild ducks—8 Charlotte Russes—4 Pyramids 2 of crystalized fruit & 2 of Cocoanut—4 Orange baskets—4 Italian Creams—an immense quantity of bonbons—7 dozn Cocoanut rings—7 dozn Kiss cakes—7 dozn Macaroons—4 moulds of Jelly 4 of Bavarian cream—3 dollarsworth of Celery & lettuce—10 quarts of Oysters—4 cakes of chocolate—coffee—4 small black cakes—

A Philadelphian who came as a bride to Eutaw, Upper St. Johns, in 1842, thus wrote to her father:

. . . All the family assemble at breakfast at which there is a great variety of hot cakes, waffles, biscuits. Soon after breakfast our little carriage comes to the door and we're off to take a drive. The whole equipage is quite COMME-IL-FAUT. . . . We are always preceded by the groom Samson on horseback to open gates. . . . We dine between half-past three and four. Sister Eliza is an excellent housekeeper. . . . The ice cream and jelly here are the best I ever tasted. . . . Before breakfast, at Christmas time, everyone takes a glass of egg-nog and a slice of cake. It is the universal custom and was not on this occasion omitted by anyone. As Christmas was kept during four days egg-nog was drank regularly every morning.

Another letter, dated October 7, 1844, sent to Mr. Wharton from

Charleston, tells of visiting both there and Columbia:

Dearest Papa,

We got here safely on Friday the 4th and found everything wait-
ing for us and the city delightfully cool and *perfectly* healthy. . . . I
spent a short time in Columbia most delightfully with Mrs. Man-
ning. The people there are the most hospitable I ever saw and I
have made all sorts of promises for visits this winter. People here
think no more of asking me to spend the week with them than you
would in Philadelphia of inviting them for tea. I have promised to
spend the time of the session with Mrs. Hampton. They are all a
very generous family and just when I was there gave 15 thousand
dollars to build a new Episcopal Church in Columbia.

Big Home was the name of Richard Richardson's place near Summer-
ton, where Thomas Pinckney stopped in 1775. It has burned down,
but there is an interesting family cemetery there. It is recorded that in
the middle of the nineteenth century one of Richardson's daughters
would go to the large dairy to "supervise" the skimming and churning,
the making of the butter into large molds for the table, and the prepa-
ration of fresh milk for the black children and clabber for the pigs. At
the same time she arranged the trays, eggnogg or mint julep for the
most favored, delicious coffee or tumblers of cream, down to glasses of
buttermilk for the younger girls.

When he was a young lawyer and legislator Benjamin Franklin Perry
(1805–1886), who later became governor, took stages at first and then
his horse and buggy when he traveled to courthouses or the State
House. In 1837, between Aiken and Greenville, he "made a very hearty
dinner on cabbage and bacon, peach pie, molasses and buttermilk." The
next year in Greenville a chancellor and two other lawyers mounted the
stage. "His Honor became hungry, and your gingerbread and jumbles
were produced by me, and we all did them ample justice. . . ." In the
1840s he sent from Columbia to his wife in Greenville a box of oranges,
two dozen pineapples, two pounds of malaga grapes, bananas, a box of
kisses, etc. Later from Charleston he sent up 260 pounds of brown
sugar, 118 pounds of loaf sugar, and wine that had cost him a dollar a
gallon.

Modern readers will find that many of the recipes in this book can
easily be reproduced today with marvelous results: for instance, the
"Dish of Snow" on page 151 is not at all difficult but will amaze your

guests. However, Southern cooks, being Southerners, are individualists and you will often do better if you don't try to follow the recipes too closely but change them a little to suit yourself as you go along. The "pulverized sassafras-leaves" on page 43 may sound a little forbidding, but they are available in some supermarkets under their New Orleans name, *Filé*. "Groundnut" is the old word for *Peanut* and the simple recipe on page 45 produces the most luxurious Peanut Soup in the world.

I am a little surprised to find that some young people today aren't familiar with the *gill* as a unit of measurement: it's pronounced "jill" and merely means a quarter of a pint (i.e., half a cup). When Miss Rutledge tells you to use laurel-leaves, as on page 28, be sure to use what today we call *bay leaves*. Do not eat the leaves off the laurel bush in your yard unless you are either a botanist or are willing to risk being poisoned.

Pearlash (p. 13) is purified "potash," i.e., potassium carbonate, while *salaeratus* (p. 15) is the sodium bicarbonate we often call "baking soda." When Miss Rutledge refers to *hyson tea* (p. 172) she means green tea from China, and her *estragon* (p. 219) is now more commonly called tarragon. On page 176, *China-root* is the rootstock of *Smilax China*, and *eringo-root* is the root of the sea holly, *Eryngium maritimum*, once supposed to be aphrodisiac. The *shaddock* of page 161 is a grapefruit, although our modern grapefruit has been developed by systematic horticulture into something slightly different from the fruit Miss Rutledge was preserving.

I assure you that when you are told to "brown it with a salamander" (p. 75) she's not telling you to bake a lizard, though I daresay some of them are edible. When we brown something under our broilers, we forget that we are doing something no one could do before this century. In the old days, if you wanted the heat to be above what you were cooking you heated an iron plate very hot and slid it onto a frame, which your dish went under. You called the device a *salamander*, in reference to the old superstition that salamanders are not harmed by fire.

What we today call crackers used to be called *sailor's biscuits* because they kept well on long voyages. Modern crackers are usually heavily salted but Miss Rutledge meant plain crackers (she is generally sparing with the saltshaker). If you have trouble finding plain crackers, the Jewish matzoh is identical and is sometimes easier to get. If you come across "egg matzohs," they make even better soup thickeners.

AWR
July 4, 1979

THE

CAROLINA HOUSEWIFE,

OR

HOUSE AND HOME:

BY A

LADY OF CHARLESTON.

W. R. BABCOCK & CO.
CHARLESTON, S. C.
1847

Stavely & M'Calla, Printers.
No. 12 Pear Street, Philadelphia.

PREFACE.

HOUSE AND HOME.

WE call this "House and Home," because a house is not a home, though inhabited, unless there preside over its daily meals a spirit of order, and a certain knowledge of the manner in which food is to be prepared and served. We can hardly call that house a home to which a man dares not carry a friend without previous notice to his wife or daughter, for fear of finding an ill-dressed, ill-served dinner, together with looks of dismay at the intrusion.

Among some valuable receipts given us by an experienced housekeeper, we find one for throwing an illusion over an indifferent dinner, to which company is suddenly brought home, by that notoriously thoughtless person, the husband. It runs thus: "A clean table-cloth and a smiling countenance." The former may be commanded: but there *are* dinners over which the mistress of the house cannot smile ; they are too bad for dissimulation ; the dinner is eaten in confusion of face by all parties, and the memory of it does not speedily die. Much of the discomfort of this might be spared, were our grandmothers' Receipt Books so studied as to make it easy to teach the cook to send up the simplest meal properly dressed, and good of its kind. But the manuscript, in which is gathered a whole lifetime's experience, cannot be in the possession of more than one family in ten. It rarely happens that more than one woman in three generations takes the pains to collect and arrange receipts ; and if her descendants are many, the greater part lose the benefit of her instructions.

French or English Cookery Books are to be found in every book-store ; but these are for French or English servants, and almost always require an apparatus either beyond our reach or too complicated for our native cooks.

The " Carolina Housewife " will contain principally receipts for dishes that have been made in our own homes, and with no more elaborate *abattrie de cuisine* than that belonging to families of moderate income : even those dishes lately introduced among us have been successfully made by our own cooks.

This volume, though not large, contains upwards of five hundred and fifty receipts. It was not thought necessary to add to its size by giving directions for roasting, boiling, baking, broiling and frying, as these are found in Miss Leslie's excellent " Directions for Cookery," and in many others of a similar character. The one now offered is (as it professes to be) a selection from the family receipt books of friends and acquaintances, who have kindly placed their manuscripts at the disposal of the editor. It is believed that the receipts are original, except a few translated from the French and German, which, as they are very good and little known, it is hoped, will add to the value of the book.

In this work are to be found nearly a hundred dishes in which rice or corn form a part of the ingredients.

INDEX.

~~~~~~~~~~~~~~~~~~~~

BREAKFAST BREADS, CAKES, ETC.

1*

ICES.

TEA CAKES, ETC.

MISCELLANEOUS.

BREAKFAST.

BREADS, CAKES, ETC.

TAKE as much hops as you can grasp in your hand; put to them a quart of water and two good sized Irish potatoes, washed clean and unpeeled, which, to facilitate their quick boiling, had better be cut up. Let them all boil together until the potatoes are well cooked. Then take the potatoes out, mash them up, skins and all, and put them again with the hops. After stirring this well together, pass it through a sieve, as dry as you can from the hops. While the liquor is hot sweeten it well with the best brown sugar, to prevent the yeast being dark coloured. When the mixture is nearly cold add two table-spoonfuls of wheat flour, previously rubbed smooth with a little of the liquor, and then mix the whole. It ought to turn out near a quart of yeast. Bottle it rather loosely at first, but when the fermentation begins, cork it tight and tie down the cork. When made in the morning it will be fit to use at night, if attention is paid to these directions. A gill of this yeast is sufficient for a quart and a pint of flour.

FOR YEAST.

To a quart of strong hop tea add a spoonful of flour, a spoonful of corn flour, and a spoonful of brown sugar; stir them well in, and bottle the mixture, which must be closely corked, and the cork tied down. Set in a warm place until it ferments. The hop tea must be cold before the other ingredients are added.

TO MAKE YEAST BISCUITS.

Fill a pint mug with hops, and cover them with boiling water; let it stand until quite strong; mix in three table-spoonfuls of brewers yeast, and two table-spoonfuls of honey; also, as much wheat flour as will make it tolerably stiff. Set it to rise; and when risen, pound in a sufficient quantity of fine dry rice flour, to cut into biscuits. Put them to dry in the shade, and keep them hung up in a bag. Each buiscuit to be a size larger than a dollar.

CAROLINA RICE AND WHEAT BREAD.

Simmer one pound of rice in two quarts of water until it is quite soft; when it is cool enough, mix it well with four pounds of flour, yeast and salt as for other bread; of yeast, four large spoonfuls. Let it rise before the fire. Some of the flour should be reserved to make the loaves. If the rice swell greatly, and requires more water, add as much as you think proper.

WEENEE RICE BREAD.

A table-spoonful of rice boiled to a pap; while hot, stir into it a large table-spoonful of butter; then add a gill and a half of milk or cream, and four table-spoon-fuls of very light yeast. Rub these ingredients well together, and stir in gradually two quarts of rice flour; salt to the taste. Pour the mixture into a well greased pan, and set it to rise; when quite light, bake in a moderate oven until quite brown.

ASHLEY RICE BREAD.

Stir one table-spoonful of butter into a pint of rice flour; beat light two eggs, two tea-spoonfuls of salt; add them to the flour and butter; one half of an yeast powder; dissolve the tartaric acid in water, and the soda in a pint of milk; stir them quickly together, and bake the mixture immediately.

The lid of the oven should be heated, as well as the bottom.

BEAUFORT RICE BREAD.

A pint of boiled rice, half a pint of hommony, three pints of rice flour; mix with water enough to make a thick batter; add a tea-cup of yeast and a tea-spoon-ful of pearlash. Leave the mixture to rise for eight or ten hours, and bake in a deep pan.

POTATO AND RICE BREAD.

One quart of rice flour, one table-spoonful of mashed sweet potato, one table-spoonful of butter, mixed with half a pint of yeast and a pint of milk. Bake in a pan, and in a moderate oven.

2

LOAF RICE BREAD.

A pint of rice flour, three eggs, a spoonful of butter, a salt-spoonful of salt. Beat the eggs quite light; stir in the butter, flour and salt. Dissolve an yeast-powder in a little warm water; mix it well with the other ingredients; pour it into the pan, and place it immediately in the oven. This bread requires nearly an hour's baking.

RICE OVEN-BREAD.

One-fourth of a pound of rice, boiled very soft; three-fourths of a pound of wheat flour; one gill of yeast; one gill of milk, and a little salt. Bake in a pan.

RICE SPIDER-BREAD.

A cup of rice boiled soft, two cups of flour, three eggs. Let the rice be cold, then beat the flour and rice together; add the eggs; beat the mixture well, and bake in a hot spider.

RICE BREAKFAST-BREAD.

Half a pint of very soft boiled rice, half a pint of rice flour, two eggs, a little butter, milk and salt. Mix and bake in a pan.

RICE COOKEES.

One pint of soft boiled rice. Add as much rice

flour as will make a batter stiff enough to be made into cakes. Fry them in nice lard. Salt to the taste.

RICE-DROPS.

Half a pint of hommony, half a pint of milk, a pint of rice flour, two eggs, a large table-spoonful of butter, and a little salt. Beat all well together, and drop on tin sheets. Corn flour may be used instead of rice.

RICE SLAP-JACKS.

Two eggs, two cups of milk, two of rice flour, two of soft boiled rice. Mix all well together, and bake in a pan or griddle.

RICE CRUMPETS.

One pint and a half of rice flour, one pint of milk, a large dessert-spoonful of butter, four dessert-spoonfuls of yeast, salt to the taste. Stir these ingredients well together, and set the mixture in a covered vessel to rise, in a warm place. Just before baking, stir in half a tea-spoonful of salæratus, dissolved in a little water. Bake on a griddle.

RICE GRIDDLES.

Boil soft one gill of rice; while hot, stir into it a dessert-spoonful of butter. Beat two eggs very light, and mix them with the rice, after it becomes cold.— Add one gill of rice flour and half a pint of milk.

Stir all together just before baking. Bake quickly in a hot griddle, and the cakes will rise much.

PHILPY.

One gill of rice; boil it, and when cold rub it smooth with a spoon. Moisten with water a gill of rice flour, and mix it into the boiled rice. Beat one egg very light, and stir it well into the mixture. If too stiff, add a spoonful or two of milk. Bake it on a shallow tin plate. Split and butter it when ready to serve.

RICE JOURNEY, OR JOHNNY CAKE.

Half a pint of soft boiled rice, with just rice flour enough to make the batter stick on the board. Salt to the taste. Spread it on the board thick or thin, as it is wanted. Baste it with cream, milk or butter, cream is best. Set it before a hot fire, and let it bake until nicely browned. Slip a thread under, to disengage it from the board, and bake the other side in the same manner, basting all the time it is baking.

RICE MUFFINS.

To half a pint of rice, boiled soft, add a tea-cup full of milk, three eggs well beaten, one spoonful of butter; add as much wheat flour as will make it the thickness of pound-cake. Drop them about the oven. They do not require turning.

RICE EGG-CAKE.

To half a cup of rice flour, boiled stiff, add a large spoonful of butter. When cold, add three eggs, well beaten, and a cup of rice flour. Drop it on tin sheets, and bake quickly.

RICE WAFFLES.

Boil a small tea-cup of coarse rice flour (or rice) to a pap, and add to it a pint of fine rice flour, a half pint of milk, a half pint of water, and a little salt.— Heat your iron, and grease it with a little lard; then pour in the batter, and bake the waffle of a light brown.

RICE WAFFLES. No. 2.

A tea-cup of rice flour, two large spoonfuls of beaten rice, boiled to a pap, a small tea-cup of milk, and one egg. This will bake four waffles.

RICE AND WHEAT FLOUR WAFFLES.

Waffles are very good when made of a thin batter composed of soft boiled rice and a small proportion of either wheat or rice flour, with a spoonful of butter.

RICE WAFERS.

One pint of rice flour, one gill of milk, and one of water, a dessert-spoonful of butter, and a little salt.— Bake of a light brown.

2*

RICE WAFERS. No. 2.

To a pint of warm water, put a pint of rice flour, and a tea-spoonful of salt. This will make two dozen wafers.

ALABAMA RICE CAKES.

Six table-spoonsful of cold hommony; six of rice flour; a dessert-spoonful of butter, and an egg. Thin this with a little milk, and bake on tin sheets.

SOFT RICE CAKES.

Melt a quarter of a pound of butter or lard in a quart of sweet milk. Beat two eggs light; add as much rice flour as will make it into a batter; mix with it half a tea-cupful of yeast, and a little salt. When light, bake on a griddle, like buckwheat cakes.

RICE CAKES. No. 1.

Take one pint of soft boiled rice, half a pint of milk or water, and twelve spoonfuls of rice flour. Divide into small cakes, and bake in a quick oven.

RICE CAKES. No. 2.

Three eggs, a table-spoonful of butter, and one of cream, half a pint of milk, the same of hommony, and six or seven table-spoonfuls of rice flour. All the ingredients to be well rubbed up in a marble mortar, and baked on tin sheets.

RICE CAKES. No. 3.

One pint of soft-boiled rice, a tea-spoonful of butter, an egg, half a pint of milk, and half a pint of rice flour ; salt to the taste. Beat all well together, and bake in patties.

RICE CAKES. No. 4.

Beat three eggs well, and add one quart of milk and a table-spoonful of wheat flour, a little butter and salt ; then stir in as much rice flour as will make a thin batter. Add a tea-cup of yeast ; set it to rise, and bake on a griddle, when light.

RICE BISCUITS.

Boil soft half a pint of rice ; when cold, add to it half a pint of rice flour, a spoonful of fresh butter, half a pint of milk, and sufficient salt. Mix all well together, and drop it in large spoonfuls on tin sheets in the oven. Bake till brown, and thoroughly.

ESPETANGA CORN BREAD.

Boil three sweet potatoes of the common size, (four, if not very sweet,) and mash them up with a large spoonful of butter. To this, add a tea-spoonful of salt, and an egg. When these have been well mixed, put in about three quarters of a pint of corn flour, and beat the whole together, adding by degrees about three gills of milk. While this is preparing, the cover of a dutch-oven must be heated, and when the mixture is ready, which will be in ten miuutes, it must be put into a skillet, which has been previously greased, and placed on hot coals to receive it. The cover must then be put over, with hot coals on the top. It will take about a quarter of an hour to bake, which must be done as soon as the mixture is prepared, or it will become hard.

With sugar, wine, and butter as sauce, it makes a good pudding.

CAMP CORN BREAD.

To half a pint of hot hommony, add a large spoonful of butter, a salt-spoonful of salt, and a large tea-cup of milk. Mix these ingredients well together, and add as much corn meal as will bring it to a proper consistency for baking. Let it remain for some hours in this state, before baking.

OWENDAW CORN BREAD.

Take about two tea-cups of hommony, and while hot mix with it a very large spoonful of butter (good lard will do); beat four eggs very light, and stir them into the hommony ; next add about a pint of milk, gradually stirred in ; and lastly, half pint of corn meal. The batter should be of the consistency of a rich boiled custard ; if thicker, add a little more milk. Bake with a good deal of heat at the bottom of the oven, and not too much at the top, so as to allow it to rise. The pan in which it is baked ought to be a deep one, to allow space for rising. It has the appearance, when cooked, of a baked batter pudding, and when rich, and well mixed, it has almost the delicacy of a baked custard.

CHICORA CORN BREAD.

To one quart of milk, add six eggs well beaten, one table-spoonful of wheat flour, one tea-spoonful of salæratus, a large table-spoonful of butter, one table-spoonful of brown sugar, with as much corn meal as will make a thick batter ; add a little salt, and bake, as soon as mixed, in tin or earthen pans.

ALEXANDER'S CORN BREAD.

Take one pint of buttermilk, three eggs, and a tea-spoonful of salæratus. Mix them well together, and add enough corn meal to make a thin batter. Drop it from a spoon on tin sheets, and bake.

ACCABEE CORN BREAD.

One pint of corn meal, one quart of milk, two eggs, and a little salt. Beat the eggs quite light, and add the other ingredients. Bake in a pan, about an inch thick.

SALUDA CORN BREAD.

Half a pint of milk, three eggs, one spoonful of lard, one pint of corn flour, mix them well together, and bake in moulds.

BACHELOR'S CAKE.

Two eggs, one and a half pints of milk, a table-spoonful of butter, some salt, and Indian meal, beat it well—make it the consistency of fritter-batter; butter a tin, and bake it slowly; add plenty of butter when ready for the table.

BACHELOR'S PONE.

Melt a piece of butter the size of an egg, in some new milk. Beat the yolks of five or six eggs very light, stir into the milk some Indian meal, then add the eggs, and a little salt, make it rather stiffer than a flour pudding; bake it in a quick oven, in a buttered pan, or in small pattypans. When you serve it, break it, as the knife spoils it.

GRITS BREAD.

Beat up the yolk only of one egg, with a large breakfast cup of cold hommony, mashed up with a spoonful of butter, and a little salt, to which add a pint of fine, washed, raw grits, well drained from the water. Make it into a loaf, and bake about half an hour.

CORN EGG BREAD.

To one quart of milk, add three eggs, a table-spoonful of butter, one pint of corn meal, and a little salt. Beat the eggs very light, and add them to the other ingredients. Bake in a pan, or dish.

CORN JOURNEY OR JOHNNY CAKE.

Into two table-spoonfuls of cold hommony, rub a table-spoonful of butter or lard, an egg, half a pint of milk, and corn flour enough to make the batter just so stiff as to be spread upon a board, about quarter of an inch thick. Put the board before the fire, brown the cake, then pass a coarse thread under it, and turn it upon another board, and brown the other side in the same way. Salt to the taste.

FRIED BREAD.

Three gills of fine grits, boiled soft; mix with it two table-spoonfuls of rice flour, and salt to the taste. Make the mixture into cakes about half an inch thick, and fry them in lard in a spider, or skillet.

VIRGINIA EGG BREAD.

A quart of meal, half pint of wheat flour, a pint and a half of milk, two eggs, and a table-spoonful of butter or lard ; mix all well together, and bake either in cups, or a tin pan.

CORN BISCUITS.

Six table-spoonfuls of soft hommony, half a pint of corn meal, a large table-spoonful of lard, half a pint of milk. Mix the ingredients well together, and make into cakes about the size of a saucer. Put them upon a tin sheet, and bake in a moderate oven. A little sweet potato mashed and mixed with the other ingredients is thought by some people to be an improvement to these biscuits.

NORTH CAROLINA DABS.

One pint of meal, two eggs, a small dessert-spoonful of lard, a wine-glass of milk. Scald the meal, and while hot, rub in the lard; beat the eggs very light, and add them to the meal; stir in the milk and a little salt. Drop the mixture from a spoon upon a tin sheet, and bake in a moderate oven.

CORN FLOUR PUFFS.

Turn two table-poonfuls of corn meal; while hot, add a dessert-spoonful of butter; when cold, add one egg, well beaten; mix in four spoonfuls of wheat flour, a small tea-cup of milk, and a little salt. Bake in small pans.

CORN RING-CAKES.

Three eggs, one pint of milk, one pint of corn meal, a little salt, and a dessert-spoonful of butter. Mix these ingredients well together, and bake in rings or small pans.

CORN GRIDDLE-CAKES.

To a pint of corn flour add a quart of milk, two eggs and a little salt. Beat these ingredients well to-

gether, and lay the batter on your griddle, of what
thickness you please.

INDIAN CAKES.

Two eggs, one pint of milk, two spoonfuls of molasses, and meal enough to make a thick batter; a
little salt.   Dissolve a small tea-spoonful of pearlash
in warm water, and mix it well with the other ingredients.   Bake one hour.

PORT ROYAL CORN-CAKES.

One pint of fine corn meal, four table-spoonfuls of
wheat flour, one quart of milk, three eggs; salt to the
taste. Mix the meal and flour with the milk; beat the
eggs very light, and add them.   Bake on a griddle,
and serve hot, with fresh butter.

CORN MUFFINS.

To three pints of corn meal add a pint of blood-
warm water, a tea-cupful of baker's yeast, a table-
spoonful of sugar, and a tea-spoonful of salt.   Mix all
well together, and bake in rings.   To be mixed at
night, for use the next morning; and in the morning,
for evening use.

CORN DODGERS.

One quart of corn meal, a little salt, and water
enough to make the batter just stiff enough to make

3

the mixture into cakes with the hands.   Bake in a
Dutch oven, on tin sheets.

BREAKFAST MEAL CAKES.

To a pint of corn meal add a pint of buttermilk or
clabber, one egg, two ounces of butter, one tea-spoonful of salt, and one of soda.   Mix all well together,
observing to add the soda just before the cakes are
sent to the oven.   Bake quickly, in patty-pans.

Rice flour may be substituted for the corn meal.

CORN WAFERS.

One pint of meal, one gill of milk and one gill of
water, a dessert-spoonful of butter and a little salt.
Bake of a light brown.

WAFERS.

To two table-spoonfuls of cold hommony add one
table-spoonful of rice flour, and one of wheat flour ; a
little salt.   Thin it with milk to the proper consistence.
To be baked in a wafer-iron.

CORN CRISP.

One pint of meal, a table-spoonful of lard, a little
salt ; and if the scalding of the meal should not make
the mixture soft enough, add a little water.   Make it
into a cake about half an inch thick, and lay it upon
your board ; put it before the fire, and when suffi-

ciently browned, pass a coarse thread under it, and turn it upon another board. When baked on that side, take it up, split the cake, and scrape out the inside; then put the crusts on the gridiron, and brown and crisp them.

HOE CAKE.

Three spoonfuls of hommony, two of rice flour, a little butter, and milk sufficient to make it soft. Bake on a griddle.

HOMMONY BREAD.

Take a pint of hommony boiled soft; add a tablespoonful of butter, a pint of milk and four eggs; thicken with flour, and bake in a dish.

HOMMONY BREAKFAST CAKE.

Three spoonsful of hommony, two of rice flour, a little milk, salt and butter. It must be stiff enough to bake in a pan.

HOMMONY FRITTERS.

Beat up three eggs with a large spoonful of butter; add to these three spoonfuls of cold hommony, a pint of milk, and a pint of wheat flour. Mix all well together, and let it rise three hours.

CORN SPOON BREAD.

One pint of corn flour; boil half to a mush; add, when nearly cold, two eggs, a table·spoonful of butter and a gill of milk, and then the remaining half of flour. Bake on a griddle, or grease a pan and drop in spoonfuls.

FRIARS.

A pint of flour and a pint of milk mixed together; two table-spoonfuls of hommony and three eggs, with a tea-spoonful of salt. The whole must be well mixed, dropped with a large spoon into boiling lard, and fried brown. Each spoonful makes a fritter.

BATTER BREAD.

Six spoonfuls of wheat flour, three of corn meal, with a little salt, sift them, and make a thin batter with four eggs, and some milk. Bake in moulds in a quick oven.

BREAKFAST ROLLS.

Half pint of boiling milk; stir into it a spoonful of butter or good lard; when nearly cold, add half a cup of good yeast, and a little salt; stir in a pint of flour, and beat it until it leaves the spoon readily; set it to rise, and early in the morning, knead in one more pint of flour. When the dough is perfectly smooth, make it into rolls, and set them to rise. Bake in a quick oven.

BREAKFAST ROLLS. No. 2.

One and a half pints of wheat flour, two tea-spoons-ful of cream of tartar, one table-spoonful of softened

butter, half pint of milk, an even tea-spoonful of su-
per carbonate of soda; mix the flour and cream of
tartar together; add the butter; then the milk, in
which the soda must be previously dissolved; knead
all together into a smooth dough; form it into rolls,
and bake quickly.

FRENCH ROLLS.

One egg, one cup of milk, three spoonfuls of leaven,
one spoonful of butter, a little salt, and as much wheat
flour as will make it a thick paste; make it into rolls,
and when well risen, bake.

NUNS PUFFS.

Two eggs, one spoonful of butter, one tea-cup of
milk, one table-spoonful of baker's yeast, one pint of
wheat flour, and one tea-spoonful of salt; beat the
eggs well, and add the other ingredients. The consistency of the mixture ought to be that of very soft
bread dough, so that it may be mixed with a spoon.
A table-spoonful of sugar, if desired, may be added
to the other ingredients.

MUFFINS.

One pint of milk, one dessert-spoonful of butter, two
eggs, half gill of yeast, a little salt, and as much flour
as will make it thick enough for a spoon to stand.
To be baked in rings.

3*

EGG MUFFINS.

One pint of wheat flour, one pint of milk, two eggs, and a little salt; beat the eggs light, and add the other ingredients, stirring them well together. Put into patties, and bake.

VIRGINIA CAKES.

Three gills of sifted wheat flour, a large table-spoonful of butter, one egg, half a pint of milk, and a little salt ; beat all well together, and bake in a pan, about an inch thick.

WHEAT FLANNEL CAKES.

Eight table-spoonfuls of flour, a gill of yeast, the same of fresh milk, and a little salt; set to rise in a covered vessel over night, and bake on the griddle. They require moving. Should the mixture become acid, half a tea-spoonful of soda, mixed in a little water and put in, will remedy it.

WHEAT FLANNEL CAKES. No. 2.

Beat light two eggs, a pint of milk, two gills of yeast, two tea-spoonfuls of sugar, a little melted butter. add flour sufficient for a moderately thin batter ; let it rise, bake it on a hot griddle. Butter when hot.

VELVET CAKES.

One quart of milk, one of wheat flour, three eggs, one gill of yeast; mix all together, and when well risen, stir in a large spoonful of butter. Bake in muffin rings.

WHEAT WAFERS.

One cup of flour, one of milk, the yolk of an egg, and a little salt. If this does not make the batter thin enough, add a little water. Bake a light brown.

RYE WAFERS.

Four spoonsful of rye flour, one spoonful of butter, made into very thin batter with water; bake in the wafer-iron. The same mixture, with the batter a little thicker, makes rice waffles.

RYE CAKES.

Five spoonsful of rye flour, three of wheat flour, two of corn flour, a large spoonful of brown sugar, three eggs, beaten very light; mix into these milk enough to form a thin batter; bake on a griddle, turning each. Butter while hot.

RYE BREAD.

One pint of warm water, half a pint of yeast, six middling sized potatoes, a table-spoonful of sugar, a dessert-spoonful of salt, and about three pints of rye flour. The dough must be kneaded with wheat flour.

BUCKWHEAT CAKES.

To six spoonfuls of buckwheat flour, add two

spoonfuls of wheat flour, a gill of yeast, and a gill of water, (in cold weather the water should be warm,) a little salt.   Bake as the flannel cakes.

POTATOE LOAF BREAD.

Half a pint of warm water, half a pint of yeast, six middling sized potatoes, a dessert-spoon of salt, and three pints of flour, stirred in lightly.

If the yeast is good, it rises in three hours, and takes one to bake.

TO MAKE A NICE BREAD.

Rub into a pound of flour, perfectly dry, a tea-spoonful of tartaric acid, dry; then make a batter of milk, buttermilk or water, as you please, and add a little salæratus or soda ; you will have an excellent, wholesome and light bread.

ARROW ROOT GRIDDLE CAKES.

Mix two table-spoonfuls of arrow root in a little milk ; add a half pint of milk, and half pint of mush or hommony ; beat the whites of two eggs, and when the griddle is ready, mix them with the other ingre-dients, add a little salt, and bake immediately.

POTATO WAFERS.

Take two or three, according to size, Irish or sweet potatoes, and a table-spoonful of butter; beat them well together in a mortar; then add three eggs, one and a half pints of milk, and stir in as much flour as will make the batter stiff enough to be baked in a wafer iron.

BISCUITS.

Three pints of flour, two table-spoonfuls of butter or lard, salt, and half a pint of milk, well kneaded.

BISCUITS. No. 2.

Take a quart of milk, make it hot enough to melt the butter, and put into it two good spoonfuls of butter; pour this into as much flour as will knead it into a very stiff dough; knead it well for an hour, and when quite light, roll it out, not too thin, and cut the biscuits with a cup.

CREAM BISCUITS.

Beat four eggs well; mix them with a quart of cream and two table-spoonfuls of yeast; then stir in flour until the dough is stiff enough to bake. Make it into biscuits, and let them rise for five hours. A few minutes will bake them.

VERY LIGHT BISCUITS.

Rub a large spoonful of butter into a quart of risen dough; knead it well, and make it into biscuits, either thick or thin. Bake them quickly.

SOUFFLE BISCUITS.

Rub four ounces of butter into one quart of wheat flour; add a little salt, and make it into a paste with half a pint of milk; knead it well; roll it as thin as paper, and cut with a tumbler. Bake the biscuits a light brown.

POTATO BISCUITS.

Boil and peel five or six potatoes; mash them and roll them out; knead them with a little flour and salt, and bake on a griddle. Split and butter while hot.

YORK BISCUITS.

One quart of flour (wheat), one large table-spoonful of butter, a little salt, half a tea-spoonful of salæratus dissolved in a little water. Make into a thick paste with water; turn it out upon your paste-board; beat it well with the pin; roll it thin; cut with a tumbler; prick with a fork, and bake in a moderate oven.

TO MAKE CRUST, OR LITTLE CAKES.

Half a pound of butter, half a pound of flour, two eggs, two dessert-spoonfuls of yeast; work them well together; roll them out to the thickness of a dollar, and cut them of whatever size you please. Bake on tin sheets.

BOPS.

One pint of milk, three eggs, one spoonful of butter, four spoonfuls of flour. Mix them well together, and bake in plates, and in a quick oven. They ought to be buttered while hot, and put one above another before sent in.

———+——

ZEPHYRINAS.

Mix a pint of flour with a small spoonful of butter; add sufficient water to make a dough that may be kneaded, and some salt. When sufficiently kneaded, roll very thin—not thicker, if possible, than a sheet of paper—cut with a saucer, prick with a fork, and put in an oven moderately warm. They are baked instantaneously.

SOUPS.

THE foundation of all soups, and of most sauces, is that which the French call "le bouillon," in plain English, broth; and, consequently, it is important to have this well made. The following receipts for broth, and for several French soups, are translated from a Parisian cookery book of some repute:—" Beef is the meat which yields the best broth; that from veal is tasteless and colorless. Mutton gives it an unpleasant flavor, but this may be remedied by using it after having been roasted, or broiled. Fowls add little to the flavor of broth, unless when they are old and moderately fat. For every pound of meat, add one pint of water; press it down with the hand, to get rid of the air which it contains, and which causes it to float. Put the pot upon a moderate fire, so that it may heat slowly. The rising of the scum has the same effect as the whites of eggs in clarifying. The scum will be more abundant, and consequently the broth will be more clear, according to the space of time between the placing the pot on the fire and the moment when the scum forms. This ought to be nearly an hour.— Take care that the fire be always equal. Take off the scum when it is well formed. Prevent the bubbling up of the pot, because, when it does so, the scum

4

separates, and it is more difficult to get the broth very clear. If the fire has been well managed, there will never be occasion to cool the pot, in order to make the scum rise anew. This is only necessary when the fire has been too hot at the beginning. When the pot is well skimmed and begins to boil, salt it, and put in the vegetables. The addition of the vegetables suspends the boiling of the pot; wait until it begins again, and then draw it away from the fire, as from this moment, until the soup is served, it must only simmer. Cover the pot, to prevent evaporation, and never fill it up anew, even if you have occasion to take out some of the broth, unless the meat should be uncovered, and then you must add boiling water, and only enough to cover it. After six hours of slow and equal boiling, the soup is ready. You must regulate the time of putting it on, by the time for which it is wanted, so as to keep it boiling only as long as necessary.

BOUILLON.

Having well washed whatever you mean to make your bouillon of, whether beef, chicken, or veal, cut it in small pieces, and crack the bones. To about four pounds, put six quarts of water; when the scum begins to rise, skim it carefully. After it has boiled two hours, put in an onion, a leek, a parsley-root, a carrot, a piece of celery, a leaf of white cabbage, a parsnip, two laurel-leaves, four grains of whole pepper, four cloves, a piece of dried ginger, and two table-spoonsful of salt. These should boil together for one or two hours, until quite tender. If it should boil away too much, add boiling water. The fat should not be skimmed off until it is about to be thickened ; it should boil very slowly, but should never stop boiling ; a slow and steady fire is required. The pot or kettle should always be nearly full. When sufficiently boiled, it should be strained ; the meat left in the sieve, may, if, when cold, it be washed and chopped fine, answer for croquets.—*German Receipt.*

TURTLE SOUP.

Take the whole of the turtle out of the shell ; cut it in pieces, that it may be the more easily scalded. Throw these pieces, with the fins, into the pot, and when scalded, take off the coarse skin of the fins and lay them aside to make another dish. The thick skin of the stomach must also be taken off; under it lies the fat, or what is termed the citron. Thus prepared, it is ready for making the soup. Take a leg of beef, and boil it to a gravy, cut up the turtle in small pieces, throw them into the pot with the beef, and add as much water as will cover the whole about two inches. Let it boil slowly for about three hours. The seasoning and the citron should be put in when the soup is half done. To two quarts and a half of soup (which will fill a large tureen,) add half an ounce of mace, a desert-spoonful of allspice, a tea-spoonful of cloves, and salt and pepper, black and cayenne, to your taste.

Tie up a bunch of parsley, thyme, and onions, and throw them into the soup while boiling; when nearly done, thicken with two table-spoonsful of flour. To give it a good color, take about a table-spoonful of brown sugar and burn it; when sufficiently burnt, add a wine-glass of water. Of this coloring, put about two table-spoonsful in the soup, and just before serving, throw in half a pint of Madeira wine.

———•———

TABLETTES DE BOUILLON, OR PORTABLE SOUP.

One set of calves' feet, twelve pounds of beef from the rump, a leg of mutton.

Put the above articles in a proper vessel, (say a digester) with sufficient water to cover them, and let it simmer, and skim it as usual. Strain it, and press it hard as you strain it. Put the meat on again, in fresh water. After having again simmered it for some time, strain it again; add this liquor to the first, and let it get perfectly cold; then take off all the grease and fat. Clarify the broth with the whites of five or six eggs. Add a sufficient quantity of salt. Pass the liquor through a clean woollen cloth, and let it evaporate in a water-bath until it is of the consistence of a thick paste. Then take and spread it rather thin on an even or flat stone, cut it into squares of the size you like, finish drying them either in a water-bath or on stoves, till they are perfectly dry and crisp enough to break short. Then put them into glass-vessels, well corked. Fowls, vegetables and spices may be

added at pleasure. If kept dry, they will remain good
five or six years. When you want to use them, take
any quantity, say half an ounce, put it into a large
glass of boiling water, and place it over hot ashes for
fifteen minutes. It forms an excellent broth.

——•——

TO DRESS A CALF'S HEAD IN IMITATION OF TURTLE.

Take a calf's head with the skin on, scald and clean
it. Par-boil it, that the bones may come out easily,
and set by the water you par-boil it in, to make your
soup with. When you have taken the bones out, cut
the head, ears and all, to pieces; (the ears should be
cut in long strips, the rest of the size of pullet's eggs.)
Take two or three, stew them tender, and cut them in
pieces; put all together into the water you had set by,
stew it down very tender, seasoning pretty highly with
onions, sweet herbs, mace, nutmeg, cloves, pepper
and salt to your taste. Add to this a pint and a half
of Madeira wine; thicken your soup with the yolk of
an egg. Your forcemeat for the balls may be made
with a bit of the head, a bit of bacon, and sweetened
highly with sweet herbs. Add the yolk of an egg,
roll it into balls, fry them, and put them into the soup
when you serve it up. You may put in sweet-breads,
truffles, &c.; but when the head has the skin on, it is
quite rich enough without either.

4*

EGG SOUP.

Beat your eggs, add a little nutmeg, chopped parsley, and four ounces of grated bread; mix well together; pour into the pot your bouillon, mixing carefully while pouring; then boil ten minutes. If the bouillon be of chicken, you may put it into the soup. You may also add asparagus and green peas, both being already boiled.— *German Receipt.*

TERRAPIN SOUP.

Take a large fresh-water terrapin, clean, and place it in a digester, with two quarts of water, a slice of bacon, two dozen cloves, three dozen allspice, salt, black and red pepper. Boil this for three or four hours; thicken and brown it. Just before serving up, throw in a glass of wine, in which has been grated half a nutmeg.

OYSTER SOUP.

Take 100 oysters, strain them through a cullender, and set the liquor to boil; when the scum has all risen and been taken off, add two quarts of water, a table-spoonful of butter, a pint of rich milk, or of cream; mace, nutmeg, pepper and salt to the taste. Boil these ingredients together, and just before serving up, throw in the oysters. If the soup be too thin, stir in a table-spoonful or two of wheat flour a few minutes before serving up.

NEW ORLEANS GUMBO.

Take a turkey or fowl, cut it up, with a piece of fresh beef; put them in a pot, with a little lard, an onion, and water sufficient to cook the meat. After they have become soft, add a hundred oysters, with their liquor. Season to your taste; and just before taking up the soup, stir in until it becomes mucilaginous two spoonsful of pulverized sassafras-leaves.

OKRA SOUP.

Cut up, in small pieces, a quarter of a peck of okra; skin half a peck of tomatoes, and put them, with a shin or leg of beef, into ten quarts of cold water. Boil it gently for seven hours, skimming it well. Season with cayenne or black pepper and salt.

A ham-bone boiled with the other ingredients is thought an improvement by some persons.

VEGETABLE SOUP.

Take three pounds of beef; and after boiling and skimming it, throw in four or five good sized turnips, and three or four carrots, all cut in small pieces. Tie up a bunch of thyme, and, when the soup is nearly done, put that, with two onions, (also cut up small,) into the pot, and thicken with two spoonsful of flour. This, as all other soups, requires boiling for four or five hours.

RICE SOUP.

Put six ounces of rice in a two-quart pot of water; boil for one hour; thicken with two, four, or six yolks of eggs, some cream, a little flour, six ounces of butter, with salt and nutmeg. Serve Parmesan cheese, grated, to be eaten with it.— *German Receipt.*

TURNIP SOUP.

Take a scrag of mutton of three pounds weight ; boil it down to a strong broth, with three large onions, and three or four heads of celery, cut small ; pepper and salt to the taste. Boil five or six large turnips till tender enough to pulp through a sieve ; strain the broth, and add as much of the turnip as will make it thick ; then boil all together well before it is served up. A little cream may, if desired, be added.

RED PEA SOUP.

One quart of peas, one pound of bacon, (or a hambone,) two quarts of water, and some celery, chopped ; boil the peas, and, when half done, put in the bacon ; when the peas are thoroughly boiled, take them out and rub them through a cullender or coarse sieve ; then put the pulp back into the pot with the bacon, and season with a little pepper and salt, if necessary. If the soup should not be thick enough, a little wheat flour may be stirred in. Green peas may be used instead of the red pea.

MUSHROOM SOUP.

Put about a pint of mushrooms, well cleaned and washed, and cut into small strips, with three ounces of butter, into a sauce-pan, over the fire; let them stew until they fall in. To this put two quarts of bouillon, and let the whole boil together half an hour. You may thicken with the yolk of an egg and some parsley: add some nutmeg. Pour the mixture over toasted sippets of bread. Either dried or fresh mushrooms may be used. If the former, they must be boiled first an hour in fair water, so that they may be softened and freed from sand.— *German Receipt.*

CORN SOUP.

Take young corn and cut the ears across, then grate them in water—two ears to a pint. About six quarts will make a good tureen of soup. To this quantity put about a pound of pork, and season to your taste. Vegetables if you like. It must boil three hours.

GROUND-NUT SOUP.

To half a pint shelled ground-nuts, well beaten up, add two spoonsful of flour, and mix well. Put to them a pint of oysters, and a pint and a half of water. While boiling, throw on a seed-pepper or two, if small.

BENNIE SOUP.

This is made exactly in the same manner except that instead of half a pint of ground-nuts, a pint and a gill of Bennie is mixed with the flour and oysters.

CLEAR GRAVY SOUP.

Wash a piece of fresh beef, and put it on the night before it is wanted; boil it several hours, until perfectly tender; then take it off and strain it. In the morning separate every particle of fat from it, and put it over the fire; season it with pepper and salt, and put in a spoonful of soy to color it. Then prepare the vegetables nicely; carrots, celery and turnips, cut small and boiled in the soup till tender.

LAMB'S HEAD SOUP.

Prepare the head, and put to it two quarts of water, boil it until the head becomes so tender that the bones may be taken out. Then cut it into small pieces, and put them back into the pot; cut up, also, into small pieces, half of the heart and half of the liver, and add them. Season with pepper, salt, a little onion (chopped), a few herbs, turnip, carrot and celery (chopped). Boil all together over a slow fire for several hours, skimming well. If the water boils away too much, add more—which must be boiling.

SEMINOLE SOUP.

Take a squirrel, cut it up and put it on to boil. When the soup is nearly done add to it one pint of picked hickory-nuts and a spoonful of parched and powdered sassafras leaves—or the tender top of a pine tree, which gives a very aromatic flavor to the soup.

OMELETTE SOUP.

Take half a pint of cream or milk, two ounces of flour, three eggs, and two ounces of melted butter, mix well together with cinnamon and salt; when well beaten, put a little butter or grease in the pan, and when it becomes hot and begins to smoke, put a large spoonful of the above mass into the pan, and turn it quickly, so that it runs all over the pan. When it looks brown on the lower side, and is dry on the outside, take it out and bake another in the same way, and continue to do so, until the mixture is finished; when it is all baked, cut it in strips, lay the strips in the tureen, pour the bouillon over them, and serve with parmesan cheese.— *German Receipt.*

VERMICELLI SOUP.

Boil and skim six pounds of a rump of beef; then cut up small and throw into the pot, two or three turnips, and as many carrots. After all is sufficiently boiled, which will be in about three hours, take out the beef and lay it aside to dress as bouillon. Half an hour before serving, put in two ounces of vermicelli.

SOUP WITH (so called) GREEN FROGS.

Mix two ounces of butter, one egg, two ounces of bread, (also green peas,) and a little nutmeg well together. Then take some large leaves of spinach, hold each, one or two minutes in boiling water, then again in cold, lay the leaves on a plate, put on each leaf a spoonful of the above mass, wrap it up, and put several leaves around each one. Put one ounce of butter in a stew-pan, lay the frogs in one above the other, pour in as much broth as will cover the frogs, and let them boil a quarter of an hour ; then put the frogs in the tureen and pour your bouillon over it.—*German Receipt.*

TO MAKE NUDELN.

Put a quarter of a pound of flour upon the table or in a dish with a little salt, one egg, (or the yolks of three) make of it a hard dough, roll it with a rolling pin as thin as possible, strew flour often under it that it may not stick to the table : the harder the dough is, the thinner you can roll it. Strew on a little more flour, cut it in strips two inches broad, lay one over another. Cut the nudels fine or coarse according to your fancy, and lay them separately so that they may not stick together. (You can make them a few days before you wish to use them ; but in this case they must boil much longer, and fresh made are the best.) This quantity put into two quarts of boiling broth, let it boil half an hour, that they may be quite soft. You may also boil them in two quarts of milk, and sprinkle with sugar and cinnamon.—*German Receipt.*

POTAGE À LA JULIENNE.

Cut up fine some carrots and turnips, some onions cut in slices, also some leeks and a few stalks of celery. Chop up coarsely some lettuce, a handful of sorrel and half the quantity of chervil. Heat the roots on a frying pan with butter—not fry them exactly. When they are heated through, moisten the whole with good broth, and put it on the fire for at least an hour. When the julienne is done, serve it with sippets of bread.—*Madame de Genlis.*

POTAGE AUX HUITRES.

Bruise in a mortar two dozen fine oysters, very fresh and washed. Put them into some broth, and cook on a slow fire for about half an hour. Pass the soup through a sieve or fine colander, and put in crusts of bread. This soup is more nourishing and more wholesome than any other that is made from meat.

POTAGE AU MACARONI.

A quarter of a pound of macaroni, break it in pieces and throw it into some good broth, and when it is sufficiently cooked, grate into it a little parmesan cheese. Mix it in well to make the cheese melt. If you have no maccaroni, vermicelli may be used. As cheese is not always liked, it may be served up with the soup, but not put in.

CRÈME D'ORGE.

Three pounds of veal, (the leg is best,) pulled with forks, five pints of water, quarter of a pound of bar-

5

ley. Simmer very gently until reduced to half the quantity. Strain through a sieve, and season to your taste. It is very nourishing, and when well made, is of the richness of good cream.

FISH.

TO STEW FISH.

Clean your fish well, and the best method is to put it in a dish, and pour vinegar over it. This will take off the slime, and the scales come off easily. Now the cooking. Put some butter into a frying pan and make it hot; then put your fish into the pan, and let it remain over the fire for five minntes, then turn it and let it stay five minutes more; then take it out and put it into the kettle in which it is to be stemed. When the fish is in the pan, you must keep it moving to prevent burning. Dredge some flour into your pan, put it over the fire for three minutes, and pour it over the fish. Then take a quarter of a pound of good butter, and roll it well in flour and put it to the fish, adding two blades of mace, ten cloves, a little cinnamon, red pepper and salt, with water sufficient to keep it from burning. Put it over a slow fire to stew. When half done add a pint of port wine. When done, put in a dish, pour the gravy over it, and garnish with lemon or horse radish.

TO DRESS BASS OR SHEEPHEAD.

Take a bass or sheephead, eighteen or twenty inches long, put it into a pan, place that in a dutch-oven—add half a pint of tomato catsup, a large spoonful of butter, half a pint of water, salt, black and red pepper to suit your taste. Cook it over a quick fire, and serve it up with the dressing. Smaller fish may be dressed in the same manner; proportioning the quantity to the size of the fish, and using instead of a dutch-oven, an a la blaise or chafing dish.

TO CAVEACH MACKEREL.

Cut your mackerel into round pieces and wipe them dry. Divide one into four or six pieces. To six mackerel you may take one ounce of beaten pepper, three large nutmegs, a little mace, and a handful of salt. Mix your salt and spice, and make two or three holes in each piece, and put the seasoning into the holes. Rub the pieces over with this spice, and fry them brown in oil, and let them stand till they are cold. Then put them into your vinegar cold, and cover them with oil. They will keep, well covered, a great while, and are delicious. The vinegar should be boiled with a little spice, a good deal of horse-radish and mustard seed, and let it stand to be cold before you put the fish in.

CHOWDER.

Cut the fish in pieces, and wash them well. Fry some chopped onions with rashers of pork. Put the fish into a saucepan, with water sufficient to cover it.

Thicken it with three or four sailor's buiscuits, and season it to your taste, with cayenne pepper and spices. When nearly done, add ketchup and wine to flavor it; a pint or more, according to the quantity you make. It takes one hour from the time it is put into the sauce-pan ; but if the quantity is large, it will require more time.

FISH CAKE.

Take any kind of fish, and cut off the flesh. Put the heads, bones, fins, &c. on the fire, with a little water, an onion, herbs, a little pepper and salt, to stew for gravy. Then mince the flesh of the fish fins, and mix it with a third of bread, a little parsley, onion, pepper and salt. Add the white of an egg, and a small quantity of melted butter. Form it into the shape of a cake, cover it with raspings of bread, and fry it a pale brown.

TO BAKE SHAD.

Take a large shad—clean it, cut off the head and draw it through that part, as it must not be cut open. Then take the crumbs of stale bread, some onions and parsley (chopped), pepper and salt. With this seasoning, stuff the fish—then put it into a baking pan, season with pepper and salt, and sprinkle bread crumbs over the fish. Put small lumps of butter all over the fish—pour in water to the depth of two inches—sprinkle over it a little flour. Put the pan

5*

into a well heated oven, and bake an hour and a half. While baking, it must be occasionally basted with the gravy, that it may not become too dry. Any large fish may be dressed in the same manner.

———+———

BAKED BLACK FISH.

After the fish are well cleaned, take off the fins and tail. Cut it into four or five parts. Lay in a deep dish, some lumps of butter, parsley and onions chopped fine, and a little allspice. Then a layer of fish, well seasoned with pepper and salt; flour it. Continue to do this, until the dish is full. Bake an hour.

———+———

BASS CUTLETS.

Cut the fish into pieces about three inches square and one and a half inches thick. Put them into a stew pan with a little water, butter, pepper and salt. A little chopped onion and thyme may also be added. Stew over a slow fire till thoroughly cooked. Drum, or any other large fish, may be dressed in the same way.

———+———

DRUM STEAKS.

Cut the fish into slices about an inch thick. Butter them and sprinkle over them a little wheat flour, pepper and salt. Fry of a rich brown in a pan.

———+———

TO DRESS TURTLE STEAKS.

The steaks are taken from the thick part of the

Turtle's fins. Season them with pepper, salt and mace. Then flour them, and fry them quickly in butter and lard mixed together. When fried, pour a little water over them, and let them simmer for a quarter of an hour. Just before serving, squeeze a lemon over the steaks.

TO DRESS TURTLE FINS.

Put the fins of the turtle into a stew-pan; season them with half an ounce of mace, a tea-spoonful of allspice and a few cloves, ground very fine. Squeeze the juice of one lemon over it, and add a gill of Madeira wine, a desert-spoonful of flour, a pint of water, and a bunch of thyme and parsley. Let the fins smother in this, until sufficiently done, then add a tea-spoonful of colouring, and when dished up, garnish with balls.

SHRIMP PIE.

Have a large plate of picked shrimps; then take two large slices of bread, cut off the crust, and mash the crumb to a paste, with two glasses of wine and a large spoonful of butter; add as much pepper, salt, nutmeg and mace as you like; mix the shrimps with the bread, and bake in a dish or shells. The wine may be omitted, and the bread grated instead. Oysters or crabs may be substituted for the shrimps.

BAKED SHRIMPS AND TOMATOES.

Butter well a deep dish, upon which place a thick layer of pounded biscuit. Having picked and boiled your shrimps, put them upon the biscuit; a layer of shrimps, with small pieces of butter, a little pepper, mace or nutmeg. On the top of the shrimps put a layer of stewed tomatoes, with a little butter, pepper and salt. Then add a thinner layer of beat biscuit, and another of shrimps, and so on, till three or four layers of both are put in the dish. The last layer must be of biscuit. Bake, and brown the whole.

TO DRESS SHRIMPS.

Take shrimps or prawns, and keep them until their feet and beards become red, as they are then tender; boil and pick them. Pound a third part of them in a mortar, and place the whole in an à lá blaise. To every half pint of shrimps put a table-spoonful of butter, and add salt and black and red pepper. When the gravy becomes of a pinkish hue, it is sufficiently cooked. If thoroughly dressed, it will keep for a couple of days, and may be heated by placing the dish in boiling water.

Crabs may also be dressed in this manner.

TO STEW CRABS.

Take three or four crabs, pick the meat out of the body and claws; take care that no spongy part be left among it, or any of the shell. Put this meat into a stew-pan, with a little white wine, some pepper and salt, and a little grated nutmeg. Heat all this together, and then put in some crumbs of bread, the yolks of two eggs break up, and one spoonful of vinegar;

stir all well together; make some toasted sippets, lay them on a plate, and pour in the crabs. Send it up hot.

—•—

STEWED OYSTERS.

Drain the water from a quart of oysters, and season them with pepper, salt, and a little mace; beat up a table-spoonful of flour with two or three of cream, until quite light, and mix with the oysters while the latter are stewing.

—•—

CREAM OYSTERS.

Five hundred of the largest and finest oysters. Lift them out of the liquor, one at a time; lay them in a deep pan; strain the liquor; take the half of it and boil it. Have ready three quarters of a pound of the best butter, divided into lumps, and each slightly rolled in a little flour, which add to the boiling liquor; and when they are melted, stir the whole well, and put in the oysters. As soon as they come to a boil, take them out. Then add three pints of cream very gradually to the liquor, stirring all the time, and give it another boil, seasoning it with nutmeg or pepper. When it has boiled again, return the oysters to it, and simmer them a few minutes, just long enough to heat them.

—•—

TO DRESS OYSTERS IN CREAM.

To a quart of oysters, after draining the water from them, add half a pint of cream, a table-spoonful of butter, salt, black pepper and red. Place the whole in an à lá blaise dish; when nearly done, thicken it with wheat flour, and serve it up hot.

FRIED OYSTERS.

Take 100 oysters; dry them in a coarse towel. Beat very light the yolks of four eggs; add some bread-crumbs or powdered-biscuit, pepper, salt, and a little mace; stir these well together, and dip your oysters into the mixture; fry them in boiling butter till they become a light brown. Corn meal may be substituted for the bread or biscuit.

TO BATTER OYSTERS.

Make a light batter of three eggs, a desert-spoonful of butter, a little wheat flour, pepper and salt to the taste. Drain your oysters from the liquor, and stir them into the batter; then drop the mixture from a ladle into boiling lard, and let the fritters cook until they are of a rich brown. This batter is sufficient for a quart of oysters.

OYSTER PIE.

Drain the oysters from their liquor and rinse them; sprinkle them well with corn and wheat flour, mixed; season with black pepper and salt; fry them a little with an onion, sliced very thin; strain, and boil the liquor till clear, and, if necessary, add salt. When ready, to put the oysters to bake, make a crust, and line your dish with it; stir the liquor in with the oysters, and put them on your crust; cover the top with butter and some spice; and lastly, sprinkle with powdered biscuit, or bread crumb, or a crust may be put over the top.

SCALLOP'D OYSTERS.

Take a quart of large oysters, and drain them from the liquor. Get some scallop shells, either real ones or of tin, butter them, put in a layer of grated bread or biscuit, then one of oysters, which must be first seasoned with pepper, salt, and a little mace or nutmeg. Then put over the oysters small pieces of butter, then another layer of bread or biscuit, and so on, until the shell is full, taking care that the bread is always the last layer. Then pour into the shell as much of the liquor as it will hold. Bake, of a light brown.

TO PREPARE MULLET-ROES FOR TABLE.

Make a strong pickle of salt and water; put your roes into a stone jar, and pour the pickle over them. Let them remain in it till they become quite soft to the touch (about ten days). Before being dressed, the roes must be taken out of the pickle, and soaked in cold soft water several hours. Then par-boil and broil them on a gridiron. Pour a little melted butter over them as soon as they are taken up.

Care should be taken to pickle at one time no more than are expected to be consumed in ten days, or a fortnight, as they are liable to fall to pieces, if kept longer.

—⸱—

TO MAKE A CAVEAR OF MULLET-ROES.

One pound and a quarter of the largest roes to be had, picked clean of the strings and skins. Par-boil them in strong salt and water. Powder and sift them very fine. Of black pepper and allspice each one-fourth of an ounce; ot mace and cloves, one-fourth of an ounce each, and one nutmeg.

Take one-third part of the roe, and pound it in a mortar, till it becomes smooth, adding the spice by degrees, till they are properly mixed. Take it out and put it into a large dish, with the unbeat roe and one pound of butter; incorporate the whole well together, adding salt to your taste. When thus prepared, put it into small pots, and bake it. When cold, pour melted butter over, and tie it up close. It may be eaten with oil and vinegar.

The roes are in perfection in November.

MEATS.

AFTER boiling the bouilli in the soup, take it out and make a sauce of flour and butter, and add either capers or parsley, as you prefer.

BEEF A LA MODE.

Take a piece of fleshy beef (the round or thick flank); take off the fat, skin, and coarse parts; beat it well, and flatten it with a rolling-pin or cleaver; lard it with fat bacon; season highly with pepper, salt, cloves, mace, and powdered nutmeg; then put it into a pot where nothing but beef has been boiled, in good gravy. Put in a handful of sweet herbs, a bay leaf, and a few shallots, and let it boil till the meat is tender; then add a pint of claret wine and a few anchovies, and stew until the liquor thickens. If there is more liquor than enough, take out the surplus before you add the wine, etc. When sufficiently cooked, take out the bay leaves and shallots, and serve either hot or cold.

A RUMP OF BEEF A LA DAUBE.

Bone it, and lard it with bacon; season with sweet herbs, shallots, pepper and salt. Put it into your pot

6

(with just water enough to cover it), with carrots, turnips, onions, whole pepper, cloves and mace, and let it stew over a slow fire for three hours, till tender.— Then make a good sauce with rich gravy, truffles and mushrooms, and pour over it.

TO DRESS BEEF.

Take some of the round of beef, the rump piece; cut it five or six inches thick; cut pieces of fat bacon into long bits; take equal quantities of beaten mace, pepper and nutmeg, with double the quantity of salt. Mix them together; dip the bacon into vinegar, then into the spice. Lard the beef with a larding-pin very thick and even. Put the meat into a pot just large enough to hold it, and let it brown; then add a gill of vinegar, two large onions, a bunch of sweet herbs, half a pint of port wine, and some lemon peel. Cover it down very close, and put a wet cloth round the edge of the pot, to prevent the steam from evaporating.— When it is half done, turn it, and cover it up again. Cook it over a stove, or very slow fire.

TO POT BEEF LIKE VENISON.

Cut 8 lbs. of lean beef from the buttock, or any other lean part, into pound pieces. Take six ounces of saltpetre and one pint of common salt. Rub the meat well with it, and let it lie three or four days.— Then put it in a stone jar, and cover it with some of its own brine and pump water, and bake it. Then pick all the fat and skin from it, and pound it very fine in a mortar. As you pound it, pour in melted butter enough to make it very moist, like pap. Add pepper and salt to your taste, and season it highly with spices. Then press it down in your pot, and cover it with clarified butter.

STEWED BEEF.

Stew, in five quarts of water, the middle part of a brisket of beef, weighing about ten pounds. Add two onions, stuck with two cloves, one head of celery, one large carrot, two turnips cut small, half an ounce of black pepper, and some salt. Stew it gently for six hours. Make a strong gravy, with carrots and turnips—the turnips to be scraped, and fried of a brown color. Add some pepper, salt, and a little cayenne ; thicken it with flour and butter, and pour it over the beef, vegetables and all.

BŒUF A LA GARDETTE.

A middle-sized round of beef, larded, and put into a large deep pudding-dish, or any thing which will contain that ; a bottle of claret, and a pint of vinegar, both of which must be poured over it (the claret however may be omitted) ; onions sliced, allspice, and pepper to your taste. Let the beef remain twenty-four hours in this mixture, turning it at the expiration of twelve hours. Then put the whole into a stew-pan, and boil it slowly for six or seven hours.

BEEF BALLS.

Mince very fine a piece of tender beef, fat and lean.
Mince, also, an onion, with some boiled parsley. Add
grated crumbs of bread, and season with pepper, salt
and nutmeg. Mix the whole together; moisten with
a beaten egg; roll it into balls, flour and fry them.
Serve them with fried bread crumbs, or with gravy.

MINCED COLLOPS.

Cut two pounds of lean, tender beef into slices (it
is best taken from the rump or round), and mince it
very fine. Brown two ounces of butter in a frying-
pan; dredge it with a little flour, then add the minced
meat, and beat it with a beater till of a light brown
color. Have prepared some highly seasoned beef
gravy, which may be made of the parings and stringy
part of the beef, and which, with the minced collops,
put into a saucepan, and let it stew half an hour. The
collops are as often fried in beef-suet as with butter.

Minced collops may be kept some weeks, packed
closely, and covered with clarified butter.

BEEF AND OYSTER SAUSAGES.

Scald three-quarters of a pint of oysters in their own
liquor. Take them out, and chop them fine. Mince
one pound of beef and mutton, and three-quarters of
a pound of beef-suet; add the oysters, and season
with salt, pepper, mace, and two cloves, pounded.—
Beat up the yolks of two eggs, and mix the whole well

together, and pack it closely in a jar. When to be used, roll it into the form of small sausages; dip these into the yolk of an egg, beaten up; strew grated bread crumbs over them, or dust them with flour, and fry them. Serve them on hot fried bread.

TO CORN BEEF TO BE USED THE NEXT DAY.

Sprinkle the beef with saltpetre. A few minutes afterwards, rub it well with salt; repeat the rubbing four or five times in the course of the day, turning it every time it is rubbed. It must be well rubbed the next morning.

TO CORN BEEF TO BE USED THE SAME DAY.

Take a tub of water with sticks laid across it; lay the beef on them, covering it thick with salt. Rub it, from time to time, frequently, until the pickle begins to run; then the beef is to be well rubbed with salt on both sides. The first side of the beef that was salted is now to be turned down, and then the other, in its turn, to be also covered with salt to a considerable thickness, and allowed to remain until the pickle again begins to run. It is then to be placed on a dish until it is time to cook it; the salt and pickle to be put into the pot with it.

COLLARED BEEF, No. 1.

Take a piece of beef, (the flat rib is the best;) remove the bone and the skin in which the bone is en-

6*

cased ; lay the meat upon a dish, and rub it with saltpetre and brown sugar ; let it stand a quarter of an
hour; rub it over well with salt, and let it remain
three days in the salt. Then wash the salt from the
meat, and sprinkle over one side a little allspice, mace,
cloves, black pepper, thyme, and sage, all finely
pounded together, and sifted. Roll it as tight as possible, and tie it up ; then wrap it in a coarse cloth,
and boil four or five hours ; take it out of the pot, and
put it immediately to press under a very heavy weight.
Do not slice it until perfectly cold.

COLLARED BEEF, No. 2.

Take the gristle out of a flank of beef, and skin it
off the inside. Then take two ounces of saltpetre,
three ounces of bay salt, half a pound of common salt,
and a quarter of a pound of brown sugar ; mix them
all well together, and rub the beef well, and put it
into a pan with a quart of spring water for four days,
turning it every day. Take it out, and see that the
fat and lean lie equal. Then take pepper, cloves
and mace, a good deal of parsley and sweet marjoram
shred small. Mix these ingredients together, and strew
it over the inside of the beef. Roll it hard, fill it
close, and sew it up in a cloth tied up at both ends.
In this condition put it in a deep pan, with the pickle
and a pint of water. You may also add a pint of claret, and must put in an onion stuck with cloves, and
a pound of butter. Cover the pan with a coarse

paste, and bake it all day. Then take it hot, roll it hard, and put it to stand on one end, with a plate at the top and a weight on it, and let it stand till cold. Take it out of the cloth, and keep it dry.

HUNTER'S ROUND.

For a round of beef of eighteen or twenty pounds, half a pound of salt, one ounce of cloves, one of all-spice, one of pepper, one of saltpetre, ground together and well mixed. Rub the whole on the meat; and what falls off on the dish rub on daily for ten days. Then put it in a pie-pan, with two or three quarts of water and its own juice, and bake three hours and a half.

BŒUF DE CHASSE.

To a large round of beef, take three ounces of salt-petre, finely powdered; rub it well and let it stand five or six hours; then season it highly with common salt, two ounces of pepper and two ounces of allspice, coarsely pounded, and a quarter of a pound of coarse brown sugar. Let it stand in pickle ten or twelve days, turning it now and then. Wash the salt and spice from it, and put it into an earthen pan to bake, with some beef suet. At the top and bottom cover it with a thick paste. Let it bake six or seven hours, if very large. When taken out of the oven, pour the gravy from it, and let it stand until cold. It will keep, in winter, several weeks.

MINCED MEAT.

Take a piece of cold meat, or fowl; chop it fine; season to the taste with black pepper and salt; then peel some ripe tomatoes, and put them, with a large spoonful of melted butter, into a pan; then put in the chopped meat, and fry it.

MEAT AND POTATO BALLS.

Take pieces of cold meat chopped fine, and mix with it well-boiled Irish potatoes, which have been mashed smooth, with a large spoonful of good cream; season with pepper, salt, and a spoonful of tomato catsup. Make into balls, and serve with sauce made of flour, butter and water, with a little vinegar and salt.

FORCEMEAT BALLS.

Take a pound of tender beef or veal; chop it up very fine; add a small bunch of parsley and an onion, also finely chopped. Season to your taste with pepper, (black and cayenne,) salt, and a little mace. Flour your hands, and roll the mixture into balls of the size of a pigeon's egg; then fry them in butter and lard mixed together.

FORCEMEAT.

Mince very fine three ounces of the best beef-suet; one ounce of fat bacon; three of veal, either raw or dressed; two of grated bread; a little grated lemon-peel; white pepper and salt, and parsley finely minced. Mix all well together, and bind with the yolk of egg beaten. Make into balls the size of a nutmeg, and fry them in clarified beef-drippings, or use the mixture for stuffing.

CROQUETS OF COLD MEAT.

You may take any kind of boiled or roasted meat and mix them together, so that it is cleared of bones; make a hash of it, and mix it with a piquant sauce. The mixture must be very thick; if it be too thin, put a little bread with it; add capers, mushrooms, salt, spice, and *fines herbes*, boiled together. Let it get cold on a chopping-board or dish; make balls of it, and press them flat; roll them in egg and grated bread, and fry them in butter, brown on both sides.

TO DRESS A CALF'S HEAD.

Boil the head until the tongue will peel. Cut half the head into small pieces about the size of an oyster. Then stew it in strong gravy, with a large ladleful of claret, a handful of sweet herbs, a little lemon-peel, a piece of onion and nutmeg. Let all these stew till they are tender. Take the other half of the head and boil it. Scratch it with a fork, and strew over it grated bread and sweet herbs with a little lemon-peel. Lard it with bacon, and wash it over with the yolk of egg, and strew over it a little grated bread. Place it in the middle of your dish.

Put a pint of strong gravy into your stew pan, with three anchovies, a few capers, some mushrooms, a good quantity of butter, and a quart of large oysters. Stew the oysters in their own liquor, with a blade of mace and a little white wine. Keep the largest to fry, and shred a few of the smallest. Then make a batter of yolk of egg and flour. Dip them in and fry them with lard. Make little cakes of the brains. Dip them in and fry them. Then pour the stewed meat into the dish, round the other half of the head. Lay the fried oysters, brains and tongue, with little bits of crisp bacon and forcemeat balls, on the top and all about the meat. Garnish with horseradish. Serve it up hot.

KNUCKLE OF VEAL WITH PARSLEY SAUCE.

Boil a knuckle of veal, and serve it up with a sauce made with the usual proportion of butter, flour, water and salt, and parsley, which, in order to extract its flavor, must be chopped *very fine*.

KNUCKLE OF VEAL WITH TOMATOES.

To a knuckle of veal put a soup plate of tomatoes, which must be first peeled ; a table-spoonful of butter ; pepper and salt to the taste. Cover the knuckle with water, and stew over a slow fire for several hours. Should the water stew away too much before the meat is thoroughly done, more water may be added to prevent its burning, and care should be taken to have the water hot.

A shin of beef dressed in the same way, makes an excellent dish.

———+———

TO RAGOÛT A BREAST OF VEAL.

Put your breast of veal into a large stew-pan, and with it a bunch of sweet herbs, an onion, some black and white pepper, a blade or two of mace, two or three cloves, and a small piece of lemon-peel ; just cover the whole with water, and boil it until the veal is tender; then take up the veal, bone it, and put the bones into the pan; boil them until the gravy is good ; then strain, and if you have a little rich beef gravy, add a quarter of a pint of it to the other gravy; also a carrot (chopped), an Irish potato or two, two table-spoonsful of catsup, two of white wine. Let the whole boil together. In the meantime flour the veal and fry it in butter till of a rich brown. Then drain off all the butter, and pour the gravy on the veal, adding a few mushrooms. Boil all together until the sauce is rich and thick ; cut the sweet-bread into four ; lay the veal in the dish, put the pieces of sweet-bread around it (also some forcemeat balls), pour the sauce all over them, and garnish with lemon.

——+——

TO STEW A BREAST OF VEAL.

Stuff the veal with forced-meat, strew a little salt over it, and flour it well   Put it into a pot with a gill

of water, a blade of mace and a bunch of sweet herbs;
let the whole stew over a very slow fire about one
hour. If the breast be unusually large, more time
must, of course, be allowed in the stewing. Before you
take it up, beat up the yolks of two eggs with a table-
spoonful of vinegar and a quarter of a pound of butter
rolled in a little flour. Pour this sauce over the veal,
and serve it up in a few minutes. Garnish the dish
with lemon.

FRICANDEAU OF VEAL.

Take a piece of a fillet of veal about the thickness
of two fingers; pass through it, with a larding needle, thin slices of the fat of bacon ; let it whiten for
a moment in boiling water ; then put it on the fire,
in a stew-pan, with a little gravy and some sprigs of
thyme and parsley. When done, take it from the stew-
pan and skim the gravy, which must then be strained
through a sieve, and again set it on the fire till it is
almost boiled away ; replace the veal in it to become glazed. When the larded-side is glazed, put it
on the dish in which it is to be served, and add to
what is left in the stew-pan a little gravy or broth, taking care that this has a good flavor. Pour it under
your fricandeau and serve.—*Madame Genlis. Mai-
son Rustique.*

VEAL À LA MODE.

Take a fillet of veal ; cut some long slices of
bacon half an inch thick ; roll them in beaten cloves

salt, red and black pepper. Stuff them in different places about the veal, rubbing the seasoning over the veal also. Then take a pot, which may be closely covered; put a dessert spoonful of butter into it, brown it, and put in the veal. Let it stew five or six hours very slowly, turning it once; then take out the veal, skim the sauce, and put it into a saucepan. Mix with it a little cream and shred parsley; let it boil up once, and pour it over the veal. Serve up in a deep dish.

VEAL OLIVES.

Slice pieces of the fillet, about half an inch thick, and eight or ten inches wide and long; lay them flat in a dish; sprinkle over them, on one side, a little pepper, salt and mace, all finely pounded; roll tight, and tie them up separately. Put them into a stew-pan with a little water and butter, and simmer down to a brown gravy. When they are to be served, have ready some pounded biscuit, or bread crumbs, which sprinkle over them after they are put into the dish. It takes one hour to stew them properly. Beef may be prepared in the same way.

SMOTHERED VEAL.

Cover your veal (generally the knuckle) with three or four thin slices of the fat of bacon, and cover that with roasted chestnuts, potatoes, carrots, turnips, onions, roots of celery, a sprig of thyme, one of parsley: these

7

must cover the veal entirely. Moisten well with broth or clear gravy; cook by a slow fire, and in a Dutch oven.—*Madame de Genlis.*

TO STEW MUTTON CHOPS.

Cut into chops a loin or breast of mutton, and put them into a pot, with some pepper, salt, and onions chopped; herbs, if liked, and a little water (just enough to prevent burning). Stew over a slow fire for several hours.

BEEF STEAK PIE.

Butter a deep dish; spread a thin paste over the bottom, sides and edges. Cut away from the beef all the bone, fat and gristle; cut the beef in thin pieces, the size of the palm of your hand; beat it well with a rolling-pin. Put a layer of the beef, seasoned with pepper, salt, nutmeg, allspice, a little catsup and onion. Slice boiled Irish potatoes, and put a layer on the meat; and this alternately until the dish is filled. Pour in a little water, and put in a few small lumps of butter. Cover the pie with a crust, and let it bake for an hour.

A NICE COLD DISH FOR BREAKFAST, OR FOR A JOURNEY.

Cut a hard boiled egg in thin slices, and place it in the middle of a bowl. Put then a layer of raw veal cut in thin slices, and sprinkled with a mixture of pepper, salt and herbs, (such as thyme, parsley and sage;)

a little mace. Place next very thin slices of bacon; and continue to put alternate layers of veal seasoned, and of bacon, till the bowl is full. Mash it down and tie a floured towel tight over it, turn it down in a pot of hot water, and let it boil two hours. It is eaten cold.

———•———

HAM TOAST.

Grate some lean ham ; mix with it the yolk of an egg ; pepper it, and fry it in butter. Put it on square bits of toast, and brown it with a salamander.

POULTRY.

TO HASH A TURKEY.

Mix some flour with a piece of butter; stir it into some cream and a little veal gravy till it boils up; cut the turkey in pieces, not very small, and take off all the skin; put them into the sauce, with grated lemon-peal, white pepper and pounded mace, a little mushroom catsup or powder, and simmer it up. Oysters may be added.

TO POT FOWL OR TURKEY WITH HAM.

Pound in a marble mortar the white meat of a cold fowl or turkey; season it with mace, pepper, and a little salt. Pound a piece of ham, fat and lean, salt beef or tongue, and season it with pepper. Then put a layer alternately of each kind of meat into a deep pan, and press it closely. Bake it an hour and a half, and, when cold, cover it with melted butter. Cold veal or venison may be done in the same manner.

TO STEW DUCKS.

Take a duck, either wild or tame; split it down the back; make some stuffing with stale bread, the liver of the duck, spice, sweet herbs, onions, butter, pepper and salt, all chopped up together; fill up the duck

7*

with it, and sew up the back; put it into a pot, with water enough to cover it; stew it till the water is almost stewed away; then add a little wine and a lump of butter to what remains, which makes the gravy, and brown the duck.

RAGOÛT OF PIGEONS.

Truss your pigeons as if for baking; fry them in bacon-liquor; then put them into a stew-pan, with a large quantity of strong gravy, a little vinegar, pepper, salt, and chopped onions to the taste; stew them for an hour or more, taking off the grease as it rises. Serve them up with rashers of bacon.

TO STEW PIGEONS.

Take the pigeons and draw them at the neck; wash and wipe them dry; take a piece of veal and chop it with suet, sweet herbs, pepper and salt, nutmeg, and crumbs of bread; mix them well together with an egg, and put it into the crops and bodies; tie them up very close, dredge them, and fry them brown in hot butter. Drain them and put them into a pan, with gravy, truffles, pepper, salt, and mace, and stew them till they are tender. Then thicken them with butter and flour, a little grated lemon, and some lemon-juice. You may serve up with them, if you please, the livers and gizzards.

BROWN FRICASSEE.

Season your rabbits or chickens with salt, pepper, and a little mace. Put half a pound of butter in your pan, brown it, and dredge it with flour. Cut up the chickens, put them in, and fry them brown. Have ready a quart of strong gravy, oysters, mushrooms, three anchovies, a challot or two, a bunch of sweet herbs, and a glass of claret; season it highly, and when boiled enough, take out the herbs, challots, anchovies, and bones. Shred a lemon fine and put it in; and when the chickens are almost brown enough, put them in and let them stew all together, shaking them all the time they are on the fire; and when it is as thick as cream, take it up, and have ready some bits of crisped bacon. Fry oysters in lard to make them look brown; dip them in the yolk of egg and flour, a little grated nutmeg and forcemeat balls. Garnish with lemon, &c.

WHITE FRICASSEE.

Par-boil your chickens; then skin and cut them in pieces; put them in a stew-pan, with gravy, a blade of mace, nutmeg, two anchovies, two eschalots, a little salt, whole pepper, and white wine. When they are all stewed enough, take out the eschalots, and put in half a pint of good cream, a piece of butter rolled in flour, and thicken it with the yolk of an egg. Squeeze in the juice of a lemon, but be very careful that it does not curdle; mushrooms, a few capers and oysters shred in a little of their own liquor, if you have it. Serve up on sippets.

TO FRICASSEE CHICKEN WITH WHITE SAUCE.

Cut up the chicken; par-boil it with the liver and gizzard, and take off the skin. Thicken a little of the liquor with a bit of butter mixed with flour; heat it, adding a little white pepper, grated lemon-peel and nutmeg; a blade of mace, and some salt. Boil it for about twenty minutes; take it off the fire, pick out the mace and lemon-peel, and stir in gradually half a pint of cream (or milk), with the yolks of two well-beaten eggs. Make it hot; but, after adding the cream, do not let it boil. A cold chicken or fowl may be dressed in this way.

MULACOLONG.

Cut a fowl in pieces, and fry it brown. Cut a large onion, and also fry that brown; add three pints of good veal sauce, a little lemon-juice, a little turmerie, and season to your taste.

CHICKENS À LA TARTARE.

Singe and draw the chickens; let them swell a little before the fire; cut in half and break the bones slightly; soak them in fresh butter, melted, into which put a seasoning of parsley, skellion, mushrooms, and the smallest shred of garlic, well chopped together, with pepper and salt. Let the chickens steep in

the butter for a little while, then grate bread crumb
over them, and broil over a slow fire.   Serve them
dry, or with a clear gravy.—*Madame de Genlis.*

CHICKENS PAOLI.

Truss two chickens as if for boiling ; put them into
a stew-pan, with melted butter, chopped parsley, shallots and mushrooms.   Let the whole stew for quarter
of an hour.   Then take another stew-pan, slice some
veal and ham, and season with pepper.   Put the
chickens into the pan with the veal ; cover them with
slices of lard sprinkled with white pepper ; pour in all
the sauce from the first pan, and add a little white
wine and a little lemon-juice.   Let the whole stew
over a slow fire, skimming off the grease carefully as it
rises.

COLD CHICKEN FRIED.

Cut the chicken in quarters, and take off the skin ;
rub it with an egg beaten up, and cover it with grated bread, seasoned with pepper, salt, and chopped
parsley.   Fry it in butter ; thicken a little brown gravy
with flour and butter, and add a little cayenne, pickle,
and mushroom ketchup.

FRIED CHICKENS.

Having cut up a pair of young chickens, lay them
in a pan of cold water to extract the blood.   Wipe

them dry, season them with pepper and salt, dredge them with flour, and fry them in lard. Both sides should be of a rich brown. Take them out of the pan, and keep them near the fire. Skim carefully the gravy in which the chickens have been fried; mix with it half a pint of cream; season with a little mace, pepper and salt, adding some parsley.

BATTERED CHICKEN.

Make a light batter with three eggs, a small table-spoonful of butter, a little wheat flour, and salt to the taste. Joint your chickens, and put them into the batter. Grease your frying-pan, throw the mixture of chicken and batter into it, and fry a good brown.— This quantity of batter will suffice for one pair of chickens.

STEAMED FOWL.

When the fowl is prepared, place it in a covered vessel, which put in another, filled with water. Put some salt in it, and after it has remained until quite tender, pour over it a rich sauce of butter, flour and parsley.

TO MAKE A FRENCH PILAU.

Boil a pair of fowls; when done, take them out and put your rice in the same water, first taking out some of the liquor. When the rice is done, butter it well; cover the bottom of your dish with half of it; then put the fowls on it, and add the remainder of the liquor; cover the fowls with the other half of the rice, make it smooth, and spread over it the yolks of two eggs, well beaten. Bake in a moderate oven.

CAROLINA PILAU.

Boil one and a half pounds of bacon. When nearly done, throw into the pot a quart of rice, which must be first washed and gravelled. Then put in the fowls (one or two, according to size), and season with pepper and salt. In serving up, which should be done as soon as possible after the fowls are cooked enough, put the rice first in the dish, and the bacon and fowls upon it.

HOPPING JOHN.

One pound of bacon, one pint of red peas, one pint of rice. First put on the peas, and when half boiled, add the bacon. When the peas are well boiled, throw in the rice, which must be first washed and gravelled. When the rice has been boiling half an hour, take the pot off the fire and put it on coals to steam, as in boiling rice alone. Put a quart of water on the peas at first, and if it boils away too much, add a little more hot water. Season with salt and pepper, and, if liked, a sprig of green mint. In serving up, put the rice and peas first in the dish, and the bacon on the top.

CORN PIE.

Grate several ears of green corn on a potato grater, so as to make about a pint and a half of mush. (The corn may be a little older and less tender than for roasting.) Add the yolks of two eggs, a large spoonful of butter, pepper and salt, and the juice of six or eight tomatoes, scalded and pressed through a colander. Mix all well. Have ready, young chickens stewed as for chicken pie, or slices of cold veal and ham, or shrimps, or whatever you choose to make your pie of. Line a baking dish with nearly half the batter, put the meat in the centre, cover it with the rest of the batter, and bake about half an hour.

A nice vegetable dish may be made by keeping back several spoonsful of the above batter, adding one egg, and a little more salt, and the grains of four or five ears of par-boiled young corn, cut from the cob. Mix all together, and fry as fritters.

Also, the above grated corn and tomatoes' juice (leaving out both meat and eggs), and baked a quarter of an hour, makes a nice vegetable dish.

RICE PIE.

Boil a pint of rice. Mix into it well a good spoonful of butter. Line a deep dish with this. Have ready a nicely seasoned stew, made of beef, or any cold meat. Add hard-boiled eggs, if approved. Put them into the dish, and cover over the whole with the buttered rice. Brown it in the oven. Some persons mix a raw egg with the rice and butter, which is an improvement.

RICE PIE.

Boil a quart of rice rather soft; stir into it a spoonful of butter, little less than a pint of milk, and two eggs. Lay in the dish nearly half of this mixture; then put in two chickens, cut up and seasoned with pepper and salt; cover it over with the remainder of the mixture, and bake it. A nice brown crust will form on the top. The rice must be salted when boiling. Any other meat may be substituted for the chicken. When chicken or turkey is used, ham or bacon, cut into small pieces, may be strewed through the pie.

A CHRISTMAS PIE.

Make the walls of a thick standing crust, to any size you like, and ornamented as fancy directs. Lay at the bottom of the pie a beef steak. Bone a turkey, goose, fowl, duck, partridge, and place one over the other, so that, when cut, the white and brown meat may appear alternately. Put a large tongue by its side, and fill the vacancies with forcemeat balls and hard eggs; then add savory jelly. This last is better for being kept in a mould, and only taken out as required. Bacon, chopped or beat up with the forcemeat, is preferable to suet, as it is nicer when cold, and keeps better.

8

SAUCES.

GRAVY.

TAKE lean beef according to the quantity of gravy that is wanted; cut it into pieces, put it into a stew-pan with an onion or two (sliced), and a little carrot (sliced); cover the pan closely, set it over a gentle fire, and as the gravy forms, pour it off; then let the meat brown, turning it occasionally, that it may not burn; pour over it boiling water, add a few cloves, pepper-corns, a bit of lemon peel, and a bunch of sweet herbs; let this simmer gently; then strain it, and add the gravy drawn from the meat, a table-spoonful of catsup, and a little salt.

TO MAKE GRAVY FROM BONES.

Break into small pieces a pound of beef, or mutton, or veal bones, if mixed together so much the better. Boil them in two quarts of water, (in a digester, if you have one,) and after it boils, let it simmer for nearly three hours. Boil it with a couple of onions, a bunch of sweet herbs, and salt and pepper. Strain, and keep it for making gravy and sauces. The bones of boiled or roasted meat, being scraped, washed clean, and boiled in less water, serve equally well for this purpose.

TO MAKE A PINT OF RICH GRAVY.

Brown a quarter of a pound of butter, dredging in
two table-spoonfuls of flour, and stirring it constantly ;
add a pound of beef, cut into small pieces, and two
or three onions chopped ; when it becomes brown,
add some whole black pepper, one carrot, a bunch of
sweet herbs, and three pints of water ; let it boil
gently till reduced to one, then strain it.   This gravy
may be served with fowl or turkey.

WHITE SAUCE FOR FOWLS.

Melt, in a tea-cupful of milk, a large spoonful of
butter, kneaded in flour ; beat up the yolk of an egg
with a tea-spoonful of cream, stir it in the butter, and
heat it over the fire, stirring it constantly.   Chopped
parsley improves the sauce.

OYSTER SAUCE FOR BOILED FOWL OR TURKEY.

Put into a stew-pan with their liquor, two dozen
large oysters, and a little water ; when it boils, take
out the oysters, with a silver spoon, and drain them
upon a hair sieve ; let the liquor settle, and pour it
off from the sediment ; put it into a stew-pan with
one or two spoonfuls of flour, and two ounces of fresh
butter ; let it stand until the flour is a little fried, and
then add the liquor of the oysters, which must be made
quite hot.

EGG SAUCE FOR CHICKENS OR TURKEY.

Melt three table-spoonfuls of butter, and stir into it

the yolks of four or five hard boiled eggs, mashed
very smooth, also a little cayenne pepper and salt.

EGG SAUCE. No. 2.

Make a thin pap with a little milk or water, wheat
flour, butter, salt, and white or black pepper to the
taste ; then stir into it some hard boiled eggs, chopped
fine.

BREAD SAUCE.

Boil in a pint of water, the crumbs of a French
ball, or of a slice of bread, a small minced onion, and
some whole white pepper.   When the onion is tender,
draw off the water, pick out the pepper, and rub the
head through a sieve.   Then put it into a saucepan,
with a gill of cream, or milk, a bit of butter the size
of a walnut, and a little salt.   Stir it until it boils, and
serve it in a sauce-tureen.

OYSTER SAUCE.

Put the oysters in a saucepan with their liquor,
strained ; and a good bit of butter, a few black
peppers, a little salt, cayenne, and a blade of mace.
Simmer this gently for fifteen or twenty minutes, but
do not let it boil.   Knead a small quantity of flour in
a bit of butter, and melt it, adding a little milk ; then
pick out the pepper and mace from the oysters, and
pour upon them the melted butter.

8*

WHITE SAUCE FOR COLD VEAL, LAMB OR CHICKEN.

Take half a pint of milk, thicken it with a little flour, a little bit of butter, a blade of mace, and grated nutmeg.

FISH SAUCE.

Take one pound of anchovies, one pint of port wine, half a pint of strong vinegar, one onion, a few cloves, a little allspice, and whole pepper, a few blades of mace, a handful of thyme, green or dried, and a large lemon, sliced with the skin. Put all these ingredients into a saucepan, cover close, and stir gently until the anchovies are dissolved. Then strain and bottle for use.

SAUCE PIQUANTE.

Mix in a stew-pan a quarter of a pint of vinegar, a very little pepper, and some thyme. Boil away to half the quantity; add five table spoonfuls of broth or clear gravy; let that again boil away to half, and add a little salt.—*Madame de Genlis*.

TOMATO SAUCE.

Scald the tomatoes, and rub them through a sieve. To one pint of the juice add a spoonful of butter, a little salt and pepper, two eggs well beaten, a small handful of bread crumbs soaked in a tea-cup of milk, one onion, thinly sliced. Stew over a very slow fire, for an hour or two.

MAYONNAISE.

A SALAD TO BE EATEN WITH COLD MEAT OR FOWL.

The yolk of a raw egg, a tea-spoonful of made mustard, (it is better if mixed the day before,) half a tea-spoonful of salt. The mustard and salt to be rubbed together; then add the egg. Pour on very slowly the sweet oil, rubbing hard all the time, till as much is made as is wanted. Then add a table-spoonful of vinegar. When these ingredients are mixed, they should look perfectly smooth. If it curdles, add a little more mustard, or a little vinegar. With shrimps or oysters, a little red pepper rubbed in, is an improvement.

———◆———

TO MELT BUTTER.

Mix with four ounces of the best butter, a tea-spoonful of wheat flour; put it into a small saucepan, with three table-spoonfuls of hot milk. Boil quick a minute, shaking it one way all the time.

VEGETABLES.

TO PREPARE AND BOIL RICE.

Wash and gravel one pint of rice. Add to it a quart and a pint of water, and a table-spoonful of common salt. Boil over a quick fire for ten minutes, stirring occasionally. Then pour off all, or nearly all, the water;* cover the vessel, and put it on a *very slow fire*, and allow it to steam for fifteen minutes, at least, stirring occasionally. The proper washing and gravelling are very important.

To Wash the Rice.—Pour upon it water enough to cover it. Stir it round briskly with the hand for several seconds. Pour off the water, and add fresh ; stir as before, and repeat this several times. The whiteness of the rice depends, in a great degree, upon the washing being thorough.

To Gravel the Rice.—After it has been washed, pour upon it water enough to cover it. Shake the vessel (a common piggin is best) containing the rice, causing the gravel to settle. Then pour carefully all the water, with a portion only of the rice, into another ves-

---

* The rice will be soft or grainy, according to the quantity of water left on it when put to steam, and the length of time allowed in the steaming. The larger the quantity of water, and the shorter the steaming, the softer will be the rice.

sel (the vessels being held in each hand). Pour back the water into the first vessel; shake it again, and pour the water, with another portion of the rice, into the second vessel. Repeat this until all the rice has thus been transferred from the first to the second vessel.— The last of the rice being very carefully poured off with the water, the gravel will remain.

HOMMONY.

Sift the flour from the grist; scour it *well*, to get rid of the husk, etc. Put two quarts of water to one quart of grist, and boil until the water is entirely absorbed. Cover the pot, and set it on hot ashes to soak, which will take about fifteen or twenty minutes. After which, the hommony is fit for use. Salt must not be forgotten.

ANOTHER WAY OF PREPARING RICE OR HOMMONY.

Boil your rice or hommony in the ordinary way, in a pot lined with china. After being well soaked, dip the pot into cold water, and it will come out in a cake.

POTATOES IN CREAM.

Put into a stew-pan a good sized bit of butter, a dessert-spoonful of flour, some salt, pepper, parsley, onion, well chopped up; to which add half a pint of cream; put this sauce on the fire, and stir till it boils;

cut up your potatoes into slices, and throw into the sauce. Serve them hot.—*Madame de Genlis.*

POTATOES A LA LYONAISE.

As above, only the slices of potato are placed in a frying-pan, with a bit of butter and a small quantity of onion cut into strips.—*Madame de Genlis.*

POTATOES A LA MAITRE D'HOTEL.

Boil your potatoes, with a little salt; cut them in slices, and lay them in a stew-pan, with a good sized bit of butter, some parsley and skellion chopped fine, with pepper and salt; place on the fire and turn frequently, so that all be covered with the sauce. When served up, a little lemon-juice is added.—*Madame de Genlis.*

BAKED IRISH POTATOES.

Boil soft eight good sized Irish potatoes; mash them, and add two table-spoonfuls of butter, while hot, mix with it a pint of milk; add salt. Put it in a dish and bake half an hour.

FRIED POTATOES (IRISH).

Boil your potatoes, peel and mash them fine; make them into small cakes, and fry them, in lard, of a rich brown on both sides.

MASHED IRISH POTATOES.

Boil the potatoes, and mash them in a mortar with butter, in the proportion of a table-spoonful of butter to eight or ten common sized potatoes, and salt to the taste.

POTATOES (WHITE) WITH THICK BUTTER.

Three ounces of butter, half an ounce of flour, and half a pint of water, stirred over the fire until it is melted into a sauce. Put the boiled potatoes in the sauce, dish it very hot, and give it a taste of salt, nutmeg and pepper. (You may also mix fine chopped parsley with it.)—*German Receipt.*

TO DRESS SWEET POTATOES.

Among the various ways of dressing sweet potatoes, that which appears the most generally preferred, is to bake them twice. You may put two or three plates full at once into the oven, bake them till quite soft, peel, and put them on a tin sheet, and bake them again for half an hour. Serve them up hot. This way of baking twice, makes them more candied. If you prefer eating them the same day they are cooked, bake them first at an early hour, so that they may be quite cold, which must be the case before a second baking, and when cold the skin comes off easily.

ANOTHER MODE OF DRESSING SWEET POTATOES.

Boil the potatoes till they are quite soft; then peel

and rub them smooth, with a spoonful of butter and a little salt. Bake in a pan, and turn out in a vegetable dish, or drop, in spoonfuls about the size of a dollar, all over a tin sheet, and bake them in that manner.

FRIED SWEET POTATOES.

Sweet potatoes may be dressed, either cut in long slices, and fried in lard, or half-boiled, peeled, cut round, and fried quickly. In the latter case, they must be drained, and served up as dry as possible.

GREEN PEAS A LA BOURGEOISE.

Wash a pint and a half of green peas; put them into a stew-pan, with a bit of fresh butter, a sprig of parsley, a cabbage lettuce cut in four, and a little sugar. Let them boil in their own juice, over a slow fire. When all the liquid is boiled away, add a thickening, made of the yolks of two eggs and a little cream. Let the whole remain a few minutes on the fire, and then serve.—*Madame de Genlis.*

TO DRESS GREEN PEAS.

Put the peas in a covered vessel, with a little salt; place this in another vessel filled with water, which must be boiled until the peas are tender.

ARTICHOKES IN CREAM.

Boil two dozen artichokes; take off all the leaves,

9

leaving only the bottoms. Make a sauce of a pint of milk, a spoonful of butter, salt, a little flour. Put in the artichoke bottoms, and give it a boil up, and then serve.

CELERY WITH CREAM.

Wash a bunch of celery; boil it soft in water; cut the sticks in pieces, two inches long. Make a good sauce, with a pint of milk, butter, flour, and salt; put the celery in, let it have a boil up, and serve.

CARROTS STEWED IN CREAM.

A bunch of carrots, scrape and wash; boil them soft in water, and slice them across. Make a rich sauce of a pint of milk, a spoonful of butter, salt, a little flour, and a little pepper. Put the carrots in and give it a boil up.

TO COOK SALSIFY.

Boil salsify, or vegetable oysters, till the skin comes off easily. When taken off, cut the roots in bits about the size of an oyster; put into a deep vegetable dish, a layer of crumbs of bread, or crackers, a little salt, pepper and nutmeg, and a covering of butter as thin as you can cut it; then a layer of salsify. These layers must be put alternately, until the dish is filled, having crumbs of bread on the top. Pour in then as much water as the dish will hold, and bake brown.

They can remain two hours in the oven without injury, but may be eaten in half an hour.

TO DRESS SALSIFY IN IMITATION OF FRIED OYSTERS.

Scrape and boil the salsify; then beat them fine in a mortar. Season with salt and pepper, and mix them in a batter of eggs, and a very little flour. Drop the size of an oyster, and fry of a light brown.

TO DRESS PALMETTO CABBAGE

Trim off carefully the hard folds of the palmetto cabbage; then boil the inner part for two hours, during which period the water must be changed three times, that the bitter quality of the cabbage may be entirely extracted. When the cabbage is quite soft, pour off the water, and mash the vegetable up with a wooden or silver spoon; then add a large spoonful of fresh butter, and a little pepper and salt, and replace the saucepan on the fire for a few moments, that the vegetable may be thoroughly heated. To the above, a gill of cream is an improvement.

TO BOIL A CAULIFLOWER.

Let it lie a short time in salt and water; then put it into boiling water, with a handful of salt. Keep the pot uncovered, and skim the water well. A small cauliflower will require about fifteen minutes; a large one, about twenty.

STEWED CUCUMBERS.

Cut your cucumbers into thick slices, add some chopped onions, if liked, and some salt; let them simmer over a slow fire, till done enough; then pour off a large portion of the liquor, and add a little vinegar, pepper, butter and flour; let them stew a few minutes longer, and serve them up with the sauce.

STEWED SPINACH.

When your spinach is nicely picked and boiled, press it well in a colander; then add some pepper and salt, a spoonful of fresh butter, and put it back in the skillet, and let it stew gently a little longer, adding a small tea-cup of sweet cream, or, in its stead, a little beef or veal gravy.

WHITE FRICASSEE OF MUSHROOMS.

Peel and wash your mushrooms; boil them in a small quantity of water, with a blade of mace and an eschalot, in a covered vessel. When quite tender, put to them a little cream, and a bit of butter rolled in flour. When ready to serve up, put in a little wine and lemon-juice.

TO BAKE GUINEA SQUASH, OR EGG-PLANT.

Parboil the squashes until they are tender, changing the water two or three times, to extract the bitterness. Then cut them lengthwise in two, and scoop out the inside, being careful not to break the skin.— Season the pulp of the squashes with pepper, salt, crumbs of bread, butter, and a slice of onion, chopped fine (this last ingredient, if not liked, may be omitted). Mix all well together, and fill the skins of the squashes with the mixture; lay them on a plate, and bake in a Dutch oven. They do not take long to boil, but require two or three hours to be baked brown.

TO FRY GUINEA SQUASH, OR EGG-PLANT.

Slice them, and lay them in salt and water from eleven till two o'clock; about one o'clock, change the water, which must be again salt. Before frying them, take them out, and let them drain. Fry in lard.

CORN OYSTERS.

Grate the corn, while green and tender, with a coarse grater, in a deep dish. To two ears of corn allow one egg; beat the whites and yolks separately, and add them to the corn, with one table-spoonful of wheat flour and one of butter; salt and pepper to the taste. Lay them in hot butter with a spoon, and fry them on both sides. It is to be understood that the corn is first par-boiled.

OKRA À LA DAUBE.

Twelve tomatoes (from which take out the seeds and express the juice); two slices of lean ham; two
9*

onions, sliced ; two table-spoonfuls of lard. Fry in a pot until the onions are brown. Then add the juice expressed from the tomatoes, a gill of warm water, one table-spoonful of wheat flour, one quart of young okra (just cutting off the stalk end), and a little pepper and salt. Let the whole simmer on a very slow fire for three hours, observing that the okra does not get too dry. If it does, wet it sparingly with warm water, to prevent its burning.

A good addition to the daube is a beef or veal olive, put in at the same time as the okra.

TO BOIL JERUSALEM ARTICHOKES.

Wash and scrape the artichokes, par-boil them in water, then boil them in milk ; salt to the taste.

ON COOKING TOMATOES.

The art of cooking tomatoes lies mostly in cooking them enough. In whatever way prepared, they should be put on some hours before dinner. This vegetable is good in all soups and stews where such a decided flavoring is wanted.

TO STEW TOMATOES.

Take ripe tomatoes ; slice and put them in a pot over the fire, without water ; stew them slowly, and when done, put in a small piece of butter. You may add crumbs of bread.

TO BAKE TOMATOES.

Scald and peel about a dozen or more ripe tomatoes; butter a shallow baking-dish, and put in the finest without breaking them, and not quite touching; fill up the little space between with small pieces of stale bread, buttered. The rest of the tomatoes mash, and strain out all the hard parts; then mix with a spoonful of butter, pepper and salt. Pour it over the dish, and strew bread-crumbs on the top. Bake about half an hour.

TO FRY TOMATOES.

Peel a dozen ripe tomatoes, and fry them in a little fresh butter, together with two or three sliced green peppers; sprinkle on them a little salt; then add an onion or two sliced, and let the whole cook thoroughly.

This is the Spanish method of preparing them.

TOMATO OMELET.

Par-boil two onions; while this is doing, peel a sufficient quantity of tomatoes to make three pints when cooked (this is easily done when hot water has been poured over them); cut them up and add the onions; also, a tea-cup and a half of fine crumbs of bread, a table-spoonful of salt, a heaping tea-spoonful of black pepper, and about four table-spoonfuls of butter. Beat these thoroughly together, and set them over a slow fire, gradually to stew. They should cook never less than three hours, but the longer the better. About fifteen minutes before they are to be served, beat up six eggs and stir them in ; put them on fresh hot coals, and give them one good boil, stirring them all the time.

ANOTHER MODE OF MAKING TOMATO OMELET.

Stew your tomatoes ; beat up six eggs, yolks and whites, separately. When each are well beaten, mix them with the tomatoes, put them in a pan and beat them up, and you will have a good omelet.

TOMATO SALAD.

Tomatoes may be eaten raw, cut up with salt, oil, vinegar and pepper, as you do cucumbers.

TOMATO PASTE.

To twenty pounds of tomatoes, not skinned, add one pound of coarse salt (Turk's Island), half a pound of eschalots, half an ounce of mustard, two ounces of black pepper, and half an ounce of cayenne pepper. Add, if you like, half an ounce of garlic. Spices —such as pimento, mace, cloves, &c.,—to your taste. Boil all these together at least one hour. When nearly cool, run them through a hair sieve, taking care to get as much pulp as possible. Put the pulp in shallow earthen plates, and dry it in the sun or in a slow oven. When dry enough, scrape it together, and make it into balls ; or keep it in glass or china jars, covered.

TO KEEP TOMATOES THE WHOLE YEAR.

Take the tomatoes, when perfectly ripe, and scald them in hot water, in order to take off the skin easily. When skinned, boil them well in a little sugar or salt, but no water. Then spread them in cakes about an inch thick, and place the cakes in the sun. They will, in three or four days, be sufficiently dried to pack away in bags, which should hang in a dry place.

ITALIAN TOMATO PASTE.

Take a peck of tomatoes; break them and put them to boil with celery, four carrots, two onions, three table-spoonfuls of salt, six whole peppers, six cloves, and a stick of cinnamon; let them boil together (stirring all the time) until well done, and in a fit state to pass through a sieve; then boil the pulp until it becomes thick, skimming all the time. Then spread the jelly upon large plates or dishes, about half an inch thick; let it dry in the sun or oven. When quite dry, detach it from the dishes or plates, place it upon sheets of paper, and roll them up. In using the paste, dissolve it first in a little water or broth. Three inches square of the paste is enough to flavor two quarts of soup. Care should be taken to keep the rolls of paste where they will be preserved as much as possible from moisture.

ANOTHER MODE OF CURING TOMATOES.

Let your tomatoes be perfectly dry and ripe; peel

them, squeeze out the seeds, and put the pulp in bottles; cork tight, and wire the bottles; stand them in a pot of cold water, with straw at the bottom; let them boil for four or five hours, and when taken out, cover the corks with rosin, so as entirely to exclude the air. The tomatoes will keep a long time, and are just as good as when fresh.

TOMATOES FOR WINTER USE.

Take large ripe tomatoes, and after washing, put them on the fire in a covered vessel, letting them remain until the skins burst; then take them out, and rub them well through a coarse hair sieve; add to this pulp salt and black pepper, to season it highly; then boil slowly for two or three hours, until it is quite thick, stirring constantly towards the last. When cold, bottle it off, cork and seal tightly. It will keep one year.

EGGS, CHEESE, ETC.

COMMON FRENCH OMELETTE.

Break as many eggs as you please into a saucepan; add salt, and mix in some parsley minced very small, and some onions for those who like them; beat up the eggs well; then melt some very good butter in a frying-pan till it no longer hisses—this is the precise moment when it begins to turn brown, and the moment for the throwing in the eggs. Place the frying-pan on a good, clear, quick fire, that the omelette may be of a good brown, and yet not too much done, which is a great fault, and serve it up hot.

CREAM OMELETTE.

Break six eggs into a saucepan; add to them four spoonfuls of thick, sweet cream, and a little salt; beat the whole well together; have some good butter melted in a stew-pan, as in the previous receipt, pour the eggs into it, and take care that it is not too much done.

N. B.—This is very good without the cream, though better with it.

FRICASSEED EGGS.

Boil six or eight eggs hard; slice them and put them in a dish; boil with a pint of milk, a table-spoonful of butter, a little salt, two eggs; thicken with a little flour; make it into a sauce, and pour over the eggs.

CHEESE PUDDING.

Add to seven ounces of grated cheese two ounces of flour, the yolks of three eggs beat up, and a little pepper and salt—all which mix together in a pan; stir this well, and add half a pint of milk. Place this mixture on the fire, taking care not to let it burn; and when it has been cooking for a short time, add a little more milk and a good lump of butter. Take it from the fire, and allow it to cool; beat up the whites of six eggs very stiff, and add it in small pieces to the rest. When the whole is well mixed together, put it in a dish or deep plate, and place it in a cooking-stove moderately heated. As soon as the mixture has risen well, and of a good colour, serve it immediately.

BOILED CHEESE.

Grate a quarter of a pound of good cheese, put it into a saucepan, with a bit of butter the size of a nutmeg and half a tea-spoonful of milk; stir it over the fire till it boils, and then add a well beaten egg. Mix it all together, put it into a small dish, and brown it before the fire; or serve it without being browned.

TO POT CHEESE.

Scrape two and a half pounds of fine Cheshire cheese, or indeed any nice cheese, into a quarter of a pound of fresh butter ; pound it to a paste, in a marble mortar, adding a small wineglass of sherry wine, and about the eighth of an ounce of pounded and sifted mace. When beaten to a paste, press it into a deep pot, and cover it with butter.

TO STEW CHEESE.

Melt three-quarters of an ounce of butter, in a teacupful of cream, mix with it a quarter of a pound of good cheese, finely grated ; beat it all well together ; put a slice of toasted bread into a dish, and brown it with a salamander.

TO TOAST CHEESE.

Mix with three ounces of good cheese finely grated, four ounces of grated bread crumbs, two and a half ounces of fresh butter, the well beaten yolks of two eggs, a table-spoonful of cream, a tea-spoonful of mustard, and a little salt and pepper ; put it into a saucepan, and stir it over the fire till heated, and then lay it thick upon toasted bread, and brown it, or put it covered with a dish, into a dutch oven till thoroughly heated. Let the cheese be just brown.

CREAM CHEESE.

Put a napkin, folded in four, on a plate ; pour on it

10

a pint of cream ; let it stand half an hour ; then cover it with another napkin folded in the same way ; put on this another plate, and press all very tight together ; put a weight upon the plate, and let it stand half an hour, when it will be fit for use.

SIMPLE METHOD OF MAKING NICE CREAM CHEESE.

Take half a pint of thick cream ; stir in a tea-spoon-ful of salt ; wet a linen rag, and stir it up in it ; hang it up for twelve hours ; lay a dry cloth on a plate or saucer, and turn out the cheese, fold it up carefully, and let it stand for twelve hours longer, when it is fit for use.

BAKED CHEESE.

Cut half a pound of cheese into small pieces, and pound it in a mortar ; add by degrees the well beaten yolks of two eggs, and the white of one, and half a pint of cream ; mix the whole together, and bake it for ten or fifteen minutes.

TO DRESS MACARONI A LA SAUCE BLANCHE.

Take a quarter of a pound of macaroni, boil it in water, in which there must be a little salt. When the macaroni is done, the water must be drained from it, and the saucepan kept covered ; roll two table-spoon-fuls of butter in a little flour ; take a pint of milk, and half a pint of cream ; add the butter and flour to the milk, and set it on the fire, until it becomes thick.

This sauce ought to be stirred the whole time it is boiling, and always in the same direction. Grate a quarter of a pound of parmesan cheese ; butter the pan in which the macaroni i ; to be baked, and put in first, a layer of macaroni, then one of grated cheese, then some sauce, and so on until the dish is filled; the last layer must be of cheese, and sauce with which the macaroni is to be well covered. Ten minutes will bake it in a quick oven.—*Italian Receipt.*

———

A DELICATE WAY OF DRESSING MACARONI.

Put the macaroni into boiling milk and water, (boiling water alone will do,) with a little salt, and about an ounce of fresh butter ; let it simmer till tender, which takes about three-quarters of an hour ; stir it frequently, then drain off the water, or the milk and water, which must at first be rather a larger quantity ; mix with the macaroni a tea-cup of fresh cream ; make it quite hot, and add grated bread. This last may be omitted, if you prefer it without.

———

MACARONI A LA NAPOLITANA.

Take four pounds of beef; put two table-spoonfuls of butter in a stew-pan ; when it is brown, put in the beef, with two table-spoonfuls of salt, and cover the pan. The meat must be stirred from time to time. When it is quite brown, put in four onions, and when they have stewed half an hour, add four carrots, and a bunch of herbs; let these stew an hour, and then add one dozen large ripe tomatoes, or a pint of tomato sauce; the meat ought to stew three hours. Take a quarter of a pound of macaroni; boil it soft, and drain the water from it; the cover must be kept on until the sauce is mixed with it. When the meat has stewed three hours, pass the sauce from it, through a colander into another pan, and let it boil once. Have grated a quarter of a pound of parmesan cheese. This macaroni does not require baking; it must be mixed a few minutes only, before it is sent to table, or it will become hard. The whole must be mixed thus, in the dish in which it is to be served: first, a layer of macaroni; then one of cheese; then some sauce, and on the top a great deal of cheese must be put.—*Italian Receipt.*

PASTRY, ETC.

PUFF PASTE. No. 1.

ROLL one pound of butter into a quart of flour; make it up very light with cold water, just stiff enough to be worked, and then roll it out; put a layer of butter all over it, and sprinkle flour over that; double it up and roll it out again; repeat this seven or eight times. This ought to be a beautiful puff paste.

PUFF PASTE. No. 2.

One pound of flour; three-fourths of a pound of butter, well worked, divided into four parts, one-fourth cut up into the flour with a knife, and mixed into a stiff dough with cold water; then roll it three times, each time putting in an additional quarter of butter. Bake in a quick oven.

PUFF PASTE. No. 3.

One and a half pints of flour, and half a pound of good lard, mixed well together; add half a pint of luke-warm water, and a little salt; roll it out three times, buttering it, and dredging it each time with flour. The oftener it is rolled and buttered the lighter it becomes.

10*

APPLE PIE.

To half a pound of apples, well boiled and pounded, add, while warm, half a pound of butter, beaten to a cream; to this add six eggs, the whites well beaten; half a pound of powdered sugar and the peel of two lemons, well boiled and pounded. Put a thin crust at the bottom and round the sides of your dish, and bake half an hour.

MINCE MEAT.

One fresh beef tongue, boiled and chopped very fine; two pounds of suet, picked and chopped fine; two pounds of raisins, stoned and chopped; three pounds of currants, washed and stoned, and dried; one dozen apples, chopped very fine; half a pound of citron, chopped; two pounds of white sugar; one pint of brandy; one bottle of wine; half a tumbler of sour orange or lime-juice; some cinnamon, nutmeg and mace. The ingredients must be well mixed together, and kept in a closely covered jar.

MINCE PIES, WITHOUT MEAT.

Six pounds of the best apples, pared, cored and minced; three pounds of raisins, stoned and minced; three pounds of hard boiled eggs, chopped fine; three pounds of powdered sugar; three-fourths of an ounce of salt; half an ounce of cinnamon; half an ounce of nutmeg; half an ounce of mace; eight finely powdered cloves; the grated peel of four lemons, and the juice of two; half a pint of wine; half a pint of brandy. Mix all well together, and put into a deep pan. Have ready washed and dried four pounds of currants, and as you make the pies, add them with candied fruit.

CRANBERRY PIE.

Wash and pick one pound of ripe cranberries; add to them one pound of loaf sugar, and beat them fine in a mortar. Have ready a puff paste, with which line your dish or soup-plate, pour in the mixture, cover it with paste, ornament it with icing, and bake in rather a quick oven.

ORANGE PIE.

Chip half a dozen oranges very fine; take half a dozen more, and cut a small hole in the top of each; scoop out all the pulp; boil the skins till they are tender, changing the water several times, to extract the bitterness. Then take six or eight apples, pare and slice them; put to them part of the pulp of your oranges, from which the strings and seeds must first be picked; then add half a pound of fine sugar, and boil till quite soft, over a slow fire; then fill your oranges with it, and put them into a deep dish, without paste, having first placed in the dish three-fourths of a pound of sugar, and as much water as will wet it. Be careful to place the oranges with the holes uppermost; lay over them a light paste, and bake an hour and a half in a slow oven.

WESTMINSTER FOOL.

Cut a small loaf into thin slices; moisten them with wine or ratafia, and lay them in the bottom of a dish; then take a quart of cream, six well beaten eggs, two table-spoonfuls of rose-water, a little spice, and sugar enough to sweeten the mixture; put it all into a saucepan, set it over a slow fire, and stir it all the time, to prevent its curdling. When it begins to thicken, pour it over the bread; and when cold, serve it up.

LAFAYETTE CAKE.

Bake a plain poundcake, about an inch and a half thick; slice it across, so as to make three large, flat cakes; put in between layers of sweetmeat. It is better if the sweetmeat is strongly flavored.

CHEESE CAKES.

Put a quart of fresh milk on the fire; when it boils, put into it ten eggs, well beaten; stir it gently on the fire till the whey is clear; drain the whey from the curd, and beat the former fine with three-fourths of a pound of butter, and sugar, cinnamon, nutmeg, wine and rose-water to the taste; add some picked and dried currants. Lay some puff paste in your patties, fill them with this mixture, and bake in a moderate oven.

ALMOND CHEESE CAKES.

Blanch four ounces of sweet almonds, and throw

them into cold water for a few minutes; then beat
them, with rose-water, in a marble mortar, and add to
them four ounces of sugar and four eggs well beaten;
rub the whole together in a mortar till it becomes
frothy and white; make a puff paste, and lay it in
your tins; fill them with this mixture, grate sugar over
them, and bake in a slow oven.

GROUNDNUT CHEESE CAKES.

Blanch one pound of groundnuts; beat them very
fine in a marble mortar, adding a little brandy while
pounding, to prevent oiling; then add ten eggs, one
pound of sugar, and one pound of butter; beat the
whole well together; make a puff paste, lay it on
your tins, fill them with this mixture, grate sugar over
them, and bake in a slow oven.

RICE CHEESE CAKES.

Boil a quarter of a pound of rice until tender; drain
it, and add four eggs, well beaten, half a pound of
butter, one pint of cream, six ounces of sugar, a grated nutmeg, and a glass of ratafia or brandy. Beat
all well together. Lay a light paste in your patties,
fill with the mixture, and bake in a moderate oven.

RASPBERRY CHARLOTTE.

Slice half a pound of sponge cake, and cover each
slice with raspberry jam; lay the slices at the bot-

tom and around the sides of a deep dish or bowl ; pour over them two glasses of sweet wine, or ratafia. Beat the whites of eight eggs to a thick froth ; add six table-spoonfuls of raspberry-jelly, and after it is completely mixed and well beaten, pile it on your cake.

APPLE CHARLOTTE. No. 1.

Cover the bottom of a baking-dish with a layer of grated bread ; strew over it bits of butter about the size of a hickory-nut ; then put a layer of sliced apple, then one of brown sugar and a little powdered spice and grated lemon-peel, then another layer of bread and butter, and so on until the dish is full, taking care that the bread and butter are the last layer. Bake for several hours, in a very slow oven. The apples must be pared and sliced very thin.

Peaches, or any other fruit, may be made in the same way.

APPLE CHARLOTTE. No. 2.

Line a goodsized bowl with slices of bread, well buttered. Cut up some apples, and fill the bowl with alternate layers of bread and butter, apples and good brown sugar. Cover the bowl with slices of bread and butter, and bake in a slow oven. When sufficiently baked, turn it out and serve.

CHARLOTTE OF BROWN BREAD AND APPLES.

One plate of peeled and finely cut up apples, mixed

with a plate of grated brown bread, each mixed separately with one and a half ounces of sugar, a little cinnamon, and one ounce of raisins. Grease a deep dish thickly with butter, cover the bottom with slices of bread, then one layer of the apples, one layer of the brown bread and seven ounces of butter on the top; again apples, brown bread and butter, and so on until the dish is well filled and pressed in. Cover with slices of bread, and bake for half an hour.—*German Receipt.*

PANCAKES.

A pint of cream, three table-spoonfuls of wine, half a pound of flour, six eggs, leaving out half the whites, a quarter of a pound of butter. Mix all well together, and fry them thin. To be eaten with sugar and wine, or lemon-juice.

APPLE FRITTERS.

The yolks of three eggs, beat up with wheat flour to a batter; the whites beaten separately, and added to it. Pare your apples; core and cut them into slices, lay them in a bowl, in brandy and sugar, about three hours before dressing them; dip each piece in the batter, and fry in lard. Sprinkle white sugar over them.

Peach fritters are made in the same way.

MOLASSES FRITTERS.

One quart of flour, one gill of molasses, a tea-spoonful of soda, two of cream of tartar. Fried in boiling lard.

GERMAN CUPS.

A pint of milk, six eggs well beaten, leaving out three of the whites, four table-spoonfuls of flour, one of melted butter, and a nutmeg grated; mix well together, and bake in cups. With the three whites, make an icing with sugar, rose-water and lime-juice, and pour it over the cups just before sending them to table.

RICE CUPS.

Sweeten, to your taste, a pint of milk, with loaf sugar, and boil it with a stick of cinnamon. Stir in rice flour, till thick; take it off the fire, and add the beaten whites of three eggs; stir it again over the fire for a few minutes, then put it into tea-cups previously dipped in cold water. When cold, turn them out, and pour round them a rich custard made with the yolks of eggs alone; place upon the rice a little raspberry jam, or any other sweetmeat.

RICE FLOUR PUFFS. No. 1.

Boil a pint of milk; when boiled, thicken it with rice flour; boil it to a pap, so thick that a spoon will stand upright in it; put it by till it is quite cold, then mix with it the yolks of four or five eggs, well beaten. Drop into a pan of boiling lard.

RICE FLOUR PUFFS. No. 2.

One pint of rice flour, one pint and one gill of milk, four eggs. Boil the milk, and while hot, stir into it gradually the flour; then add the eggs, which must be first beaten quite light; drop the batter from a spoon into boiling lard; let the puffs boil until quite brown. To be eaten with sugar and wine, or with lemon-juice.

PUDDING SAUCE.

Six heaping table-spoonfuls of loaf sugar, half a pound of butter, worked to a cream; then add one egg, one wineglass of white wine, one nutmeg.— When it is all well mixed, set it on the fire until it comes to a boil: it is then fit for use.

PLUM PUDDING.

Six pounds of raisins, four pounds of currants, four and a half dozen eggs, two pounds of citron, half an ounce of mace, one pint of brandy, six pounds of suet, four loaves of bakers' bread, two pounds of brown sugar, one table-spoonful of salt. The above ingredients will make twelve small puddings. Boil them in cloths two hours. When done, hang them up in the same cloths, without opening until you wish to use them. Then boil one hour longer. The pudding will keep perfectly well all winter.

BOILED PLUM PUDDING.

Two table-spoonfuls of wheat flour, five of grated

11

bread, one pound of beef suet (picked and chopped), one pound of white sugar, one pound of currants (washed and stoned), half a pound of raisins (stoned), twelve eggs, a little citron, and one gill of brandy.— Beat the eggs, and add the other ingredients to them. Wet and flour a linen cloth ; pour the pudding into it, tie it up tight, put it into boiling water, and keep it constantly boiling till sufficiently done.　To be eaten with sauce : spice, to the taste, may be added.

BAKED PLUM PUDDING.

One pound of wheat flour, three quarters of a pound of butter, half pound of sugar, half pound of raisins, ten eggs,and one nutmeg; beat the eggs quite light ; rub the butter and sugar to a cream, and mix them with the eggs ; then add the flour, and nutmeg, and the raisins, which must be just stoned, and cut in two ; bake half an hour in a quick oven.　To be eaten with sauce.

LIGHT PUDDING.

Boil a quart of milk with a little cinnamon, and pour it upon twelve eggs, beaten quite light ; stir in four spoonfuls of wheat flour ; dip a linen cloth into boiling water, and flour it well on one side ; pour the pudding into it, and tie it up carefully ; then put it into a pot of boiling water, observing to keep a plate under the pudding while it is boiling.　This pudding is to be eaten with sauce.

PRINCE ALBERT'S PUDDING.

Two ounces of finely shred suet, a quarter of a pound of bread crumbs, a quarter of a pound of currants; shake these round the mould which must be well buttered. Then add five eggs, a large spoonful of brandy, two ounces of sugar, and the peel of half a lemon grated fine; the whites of two eggs must be well beaten with sifted sugar, and laid on the top of the pudding when turned out of the mould. It must be slowly boiled for two hours in a quart mould.—*English Receipt.*

VICTORIA'S PUDDING.

Cover a dish with a very thin paste, then spread raspberry-jam over it; beat up the yolks of four eggs, and the white of one, and a quarter of a pound of fine sifted sugar, a quarter of a pound of butter, flavored with sweet and bitter almonds; mix them well together, and pour it over the preserve; bake in a slow oven one hour. The almonds must be dried before the fire, and finely pounded in a mortar.—*English Receipt.*

BAKEWELL PUDDING.

Line a tart dish with good puff paste; put in the bottom of the dish, a layer of preserves of any kind, with a few slices of candied lemon; then add the following mixture: clarified butter and sugar, one pound each, and the yolks of eight eggs; these must all be beaten together, put into a dish, and baked in a moderate oven. Blanched almonds, and thin slices of candied lemon peel, may be placed on the top, and the pudding eaten cold.

RYE BREAD PUDDING.

Quarter of a pound of rye bread, dried and pounded fine, three-quarters of a pound of almonds, blanched and pounded, quarter of a pound of sugar, and fourteen eggs ; stir these together for half an hour ; then put the mixture into a form, covered closely, and boil it three-quarters of an hour. The form must be only three parts covered with water, that so it may not boil over the form ; serve it with wine sauce.

BOILED BREAD PUDDING.

Take a pound of the crumb of French rolls, and pour upon it a pint of new milk, boiled ; with this, mix the yolks of seven eggs, and the whites of three, well beaten ; grate in a little nutmeg; butter your cloth ; pour in the pudding; tie it up tight, and boil it an hour. To be eaten with sauce, or with butter only.

FANCY PUDDING.

A loaf of French bread sliced, half a pint of milk, poured over it ; the other half pint mix with four well beaten eggs ; add sugar and cinnamon to your taste ; dip each slice of bread in the mixture, and fry it in lard or butter. It is to be eaten with a sauce of sugar, wine and nutmeg.

A SLIGHT PUDDING.

Add to three dessert spoonfuls of flour, a pint of milk, four eggs, a quarter of a pound of sugar, a dessert spoonful of butter, two table-spoonfuls of rose water, and a tea-spoonful of powdered cinnamon and mace ; rub up the butter, sugar and the yolks of the eggs together, beat the white of the eggs separately ; stir in the flour gradually, then add the milk and spice ; bake in a moderate oven. Rice flour may be used instead of wheat.

CREAM PUDDING.

To one quart of cream, add the whites of three eggs, well beaten ; one glass of wine, and sugar to your taste. It must be beaten till it becomes stiff, and poured over a dish of sweetmeats.

SPONGE-CAKE PUDDING.

Beat up three eggs, leaving out the whites of two, add to them gradually one pint and a half of milk, then mix very carefully in the milk and eggs, three table-spoonfuls of wheat flour, and two spoonfuls of sugar ; boil it over a slow fire ; stir it while mixing in the flour, to prevent its burning ; pour it over sponge cake, soaked in wine. It is eaten cold, and sprinkled with powdered cinnamon.

11*

POOR MAN'S RICE PUDDING.

Sweeten a quart of milk to your taste ; stir into it a small tea-cup of washed rice, and put a spoonful of butter in the middle of the dish ; put it into the oven, and bake an hour.

POOR MAN'S BREAD PUDDING.

Pour boiling water over half a loaf of stale bread, and covering it up closely, let it remain until thoroughly soaked ; then squeeze it in a towel until half the water is out ; put it into a bowl, and sweeten with brown sugar to the taste ; add, while hot, a large table-spoonful of butter ; flavor with grated nutmeg, a spoonful of brandy, ditto of rose-water ; add some stoned raisins. It should be put in a well buttered baking dish about an inch deep, and should bake four hours in a slow oven.

TRANSPARENT PUDDING.

Half a pound of sugar, half a pound of fresh butter, the yolks of eight eggs ; lay in a deep dish any kind of dried sweetmeat ; rub the butter and sugar together ; beat the eggs well, and add them ; then pour this mixture upon the sweetmeats, and bake in a slow oven for half an hour. Turn it out of the dish into a plate ; then turn it over again into a dish, so that the preserves be at the bottom of the pudding. When quite cold, ice it ; and it may be garnished to suit the fancy.

STARCH PUDDING.

Boil two quarts of milk with a quarter of a pound of almonds (a few of them may be bitter ones), a small piece of vanilla bean, with sugar to your taste; then mix in a quarter of a pound of the best starch, which you must have all ready mixed in a little cold milk (a portion of the two quarts having been reserved for that purpose); stir until it boils; then take ten eggs, beat the yolks and whites separately; mix in the yolks first; then the whites, beaten to a froth; and as soon as the latter is put in, take it from the fire, pour it into a deep dish just rinsed with cold water. Serve with it any kind of sauce.—*German Receipt.*

ARROW ROOT PUDDING.

To one quart of milk add nine eggs and one and a half table-spoonfuls of arrow root; flour a cloth well, throw this mixture into it, tie it up tight, and boil it half an hour.

NUDEL PUDDING.

Boil a pint of cream or milk, two ounces of butter, the same of sugar, and some lemon-peel; add five ounces of vermicelli (crushed) to it, and soak it over the fire a quarter of an hour; then mix in five eggs, put it in a pan or dish, bake it, and serve it with a sweet sauce.—*German Receipt.*

POTATOES AND RAISIN PUDDING.

Mix two ounces of butter, four eggs, one and a half

ounces of sugar and lemon-peel, well together; then put six ounces of grated potatoes and the eighth of a pound of raisins with it, and bake it in a form or mould, by two degrees of heat, for half an hour. Serve it with or without snow: (the white of eggs beaten to froth is what is meant by snow.) Instead of the raisins you may mix in it two ounces of almonds, among which are four bitter ones.—*German Receipt.*

GERMAN PUDDING.

To one pint of milk add six eggs, well beaten, six spoonfuls of flour, half a spoonful of butter, half a nutmeg, and one tea-spoonful of salt; pour it into a well greased pan, and bake for half an hour. To be eaten with wine sauce.

FIG PUDDING.

Fill a soup plate with ripe figs, peeled and mashed very fine; to this add three table-spoonfuls of sugar, half a table-spoonful of wheat flour, and a teaspoonful of butter. Bake in a moderate oven.

BOILED CUSTARD PUDDING.

Beat light six eggs; stir in one quart of milk and half a glass of rose-water, sweetened to your taste; strain it into a deep dish; bake it in a Dutch oven, with boiling water as deep as the dish.

RICE PUDDING.

Four table-spoonfuls of soft boiled rice, quarter of a pound of butter, one quart of milk, eight eggs; scald the milk with a few sticks of cinnamon, and while warm, stir into it the rice, butter and eggs, which must be first beaten. Sweeten to the taste, and bake in a dish.

RICE FLOUR PUDDING. No. 1.

Mix three table-spoonfuls of rice flour into a pint of milk, and boil to a pap; then stir in half a pound of fresh butter. When almost cold, add three well beaten eggs, sugar to your taste, a glass of wine, a grated nutmeg, and a little salt; lay crust on shallow plates, and bake. Dust some sugar over them.

RICE FLOUR PUDDING. No. 2.

One quart of milk, half a pound of rice flour, ten ounces of butter, and the yolks of ten eggs; scald the milk, and pour it boiling on the flour; then add the butter; beat the eggs and stir them into the mixture, with sugar to the taste. Bake in a dish, in a Dutch oven, which must be hotter at the bottom than at the top. Spices may be added, if desired.

GERMAN RICE PUDDING.

Boil three pints of milk, and, as soon as it boils, throw into it half a pint of rice, nicely picked and

washed, and boil the milk half away; then mix, in a
bowl, half a pint of cream, one egg, half a tea-spoonful of salt, a table-spoonful of brown sugar, and pour
the mixture into the rice and milk on the fire; boil it
for five minutes, stirring all the time; pour into your
dish, and sprinkle sugar over it.

ORANGE PUDDING.

Take four large oranges, pare three of them, and
boil the peel until it is tender, and the bitter is sufficiently extracted; grate the other orange, and pound
the boiled and grated peel together, with enough of
the juice and pulp (picked free from seeds and strings)
to make it agreeable; then add three-fourths of a pound
of sugar and quarter of a pound of butter (melted), the
yolks of ten eggs, and the whites of two (well beat).
Bake in a puff paste.

SWEET POTATO PONE. No. 1.

A quart of grated potato, three-fourths of a pound of
sugar, ten ounces of butter, half a pint of milk, three
table-spoonfuls of powdered ginger, the grated peel of
a sweet orange. Rub the ingredients well together,
and bake in a shallow plate, in a slow oven.

SWEET POTATO PONE. No. 2.

Peel and grate two moderate sized sweet potatoes;
pour on it nearly a pint of cold water, four good spoon-

fuls of brown sugar, one good spoonful of butter; season with ginger to the taste. Bake in a moderate oven about three hours.

SWEET POTATO PUDDING.

Boil two pounds of sweet potatoes very soft; while warm, add three-fourths of a pound of butter, and beat them together till they become perfectly white; have eight eggs well beaten with half a pound of sugar, pour it over the potatoes, and beat them together; then add a grated nutmeg, two glasses of wine, four glasses of milk, one glass of rose-water, and the grated peel of two sweet oranges. Bake in a quick oven.

BAKED IRISH POTATO PUDDING.

Three large Irish potatoes, boiled mealy and mashed in a mortar; break five eggs into it; also, add half a pound of butter, quarter of a pound of sugar, the grated peel of two lemons and the juice of one, a grated nutmeg, half a glass of wine, and half a glass of brandy. All to be well rubbed together in the mortar. Put the mixture into a buttered dish, or soup plate, and bake in a moderate oven.

BOILED IRISH POTATO PUDDING.

Take one pound of potatoes, boiled the day before, and grated just as you are about to use them, half a pound of sugar, two lemons grated, the juice of one, ten eggs, the yolks and whites beaten separately; mix all well together, put into a form immediately, and boil two hours. You may serve wine, or any other sauce, with this pudding.

TAPIOCA PUDDING.

A tea-cupful of tapioca soaked in warm water, four eggs, beat up with about three spoonfuls of sugar, a good spoonful of butter, melted into half a pint of milk. Stir all together, flavor to the taste, and bake in a quick oven.

GRUEL PUDDING.

To one quart of strained corn gruel add eight eggs, well beaten, seven table-spoonfuls of wheat flour, and a little salt. When well mixed, scald and flour a towel, and boil for one hour and a half. Serve with sauce as for a batter pudding.

ALMOND PUDDING.

Half a pound of blanched almonds, finely pounded with orange (or rose) water, to prevent their oiling ; one pint of thick cream, or half a pound of fresh butter, half a pound of white sugar, two large Naples biscuits, grated, and the yolks of five eggs. Stir the butter or cream with the sugar, then add the eggs, which must be beaten light, alternately with the grated biscuit ; then stir in the almonds. Put the mixture into puff paste, and bake in a slow oven. This pudding may be made without the biscuits, but *with* the whites of the eggs.

RATAFIA PUDDING.

Beat half a pint of peach-kernels with a little rose-water, or ratafia ; sweeten them to your taste ; rub in a quarter of a pound of butter, a little cream, the yolks of two eggs, and a little mace. Lay in the bottom of your dish, or plate, a light paste, and fill with the mixture. Bake in a quick oven.

COCOA-NUT PUDDING.

Peel and grate a large cocoa-nut ; dissolve one pound of loaf sugar in a little water, in which boil the cocoa-nut a quarter of an hour, over a slow fire.— Then add three eggs (beaten) and a little rose-water. Bake in a puff paste.

COCOA-NUT PUFFS.

To a cocoa-nut, dried and grated, add the yolks of six, and the whites of three eggs, a table-spoonful of butter, sugar and rose, or orange flower water, to the taste. Beat all these ingredients well together, then lay a light paste in your patties, fill with the mixture, and bake.

BAKED APPLE PUDDING.

One dozen apples, cored and stewed, eight ounces of butter, eight eggs, the juice of two lemons and the peel (or in place of the peel, one tea-spoonful of essence), sugar to the taste. Beat the eggs separately ; then add the other ingredients. Mix the whole well together, and bake an hour.

12

APPLE PUDDING À LA RHUM.

A pound of sugar, three-quarters of a pound of butter, twelve eggs, leaving out five of the whites; beat them together as a cake. Boil the apples, and strain them through a sieve, and add as many to the mixture as may suit the taste. Just before baking, put in two table-spoonfuls of Jamaica rum and a little nutmeg.

CUSTARD APPLE PUDDING.

Pare and cut in slices three or four apples; put a paste at the bottom of the dish; then lay a covering of apples and sugar. Throw a custard over the top and bake it.

CITRON PUDDING.

Line a plate with paste; line that with a layer of citron; take a quarter of a pound of butter, and a quarter of a pound of sugar; rub them to a cream; add the whites of two, and the yolks of three eggs, beaten separately. Flavor with nutmeg, rose-water and lemon-juice. Pour this mixture upon the citron, and bake.

LEMON PUDDING.

Six lemons, one pound of sugar, half pound of butter, one nutmeg (grated), a wine-glass of rose-water and a gill of lemon-juice. Cut the lemons in half, and squeeze the juice, then boil the skins until they become tender, and the bitter is sufficiently extracted.

Take them out and drain them ; pound them in a marble mortar until quite fine ; then rub them through a coarse sieve, and add the yolks of eight eggs and the whites of four, the sugar and butter (melted), the spice, juice and essence. Rub all well together, and bake in a puff paste.

PINE APPLE PUDDING.

One grated pine apple, half a pound of butter, half a pound of sugar, six eggs, and three ounces of grated bread ; rub the butter and sugar into a cream ; beat the eggs, (white and yolks separately,) and add them; then the fruit and bread, and bake either with, or without a crust.

BREAD AND BUTTER PUDDING.

Slice your bread very thin and butter it; cover the bottom of a baking dish with the slices, lay over them strips of citron and some currants, if desired ; have ready a rich custard, and pour half of it over the bread and fruit, then another layer of bread and fruit, then the rest of the custard, and over the top put a layer of bread and butter, and dust some sugar over it. Bake it as you would custard.

SUNDERLAND PUDDING.

One pint of cream, nine spoonfuls of flour, six eggs, salt and nutmeg to your taste ; bake in cups. To be eaten with sauce, or sugar and wine.

CHARLOTTE RUSSE. No. 1.

Dissolve half an ounce of isinglass in a cup of sweet milk, have ready a pint of rich cream, into which stir powdered loaf sugar until it is very sweet, as the freezing destroys the sweet taste ; flavor with vanilla, rose, or any other essence. Beat up the whites of seven eggs, very light ; stir the dissolved isinglass into the bowl of cream after it is sweetened and flavored ; then set your bowl into a tub of ice, and stir until it thickens ; then add last the whites of eggs ; put the mixture into a mould lined with sponge cake, and place the mould on ice. The cake can be joined with a little isinglass to make it thick ; but this has not been found necessary. The Charlotte may be made in the morning for a late dinner, or in winter, over night ; turn the mould after cutting it round, and the charlotte will come out.

CHARLOTTE RUSSE. No. 2.

One pint of milk made into a custard with the yolks of six eggs, and six ounces of white sugar, flavored with vanilla bean, one ounce of isinglass dissolved in milk, and mixed with custard, one pint of cream, whipped to a froth, and mixed gradually with the custard ; stirring the whole constantly with a large spoon. The mould to be lined with light sponge cake, cut in strips, and placed on the bottom around the slices ; then filled with the mixture, and the top covered in the same manner, with the cake. The mould to be surrounded for some hours with ice, until the Charlotte is completely frozen ; then turned out as you would ice cream.

OMELETTE SOUFFLEE. No. 1.

Break six eggs, keep the whites and yolks apart, add to them four dessert-spoonfuls of powered sugar ; cut up very fine the rind of half a lemon, which add to the yolks, and rub up these with lemon juice and sugar, then beat up the whites as if for cakes, put half a pound of fresh butter into a frying pan, and place over a hot fire ; when the butter is melted, throw in the eggs, and keep stirring it till the bottom of the mixture comes to the top ; pour it then on a buttered plate, which take care to place on red hot ashes; sprinkle the omelette well with powdered sugar ; put it in a dutch oven very hot ; when done of a light brown, serve up.—*Madame de Genlis.*

OMELETTE SOUFFLÉE. No. 2.

Nine eggs, a fresh lemon, sifted loaf sugar ; beat the yolks and whites of the eggs separately—the whites first, making them as light as you would for icing of cake, then put them in a cool place ; then beat the yolks, and while beating, have the rind of the lemon grated in ; then have the lemon squeezed, and the juice strained, and poured in while beating ; then put in gradually, enough sugar to make it very sweet—beating all the time. When very light, pour

11*

into a pan, greased and warmed, first the yolks, then the whites, and beat them well together; then bake in a moderate oven about twenty minutes; sift a little loaf sugar over it, and send it in immediately.

CUSTARD.

A quart of milk, and five eggs, half a pound of sugar; beat the yolks, and the sugar together well, add the whites beaten very hard, put some cinnamon in the milk, and when it boils, pour it slowly into the eggs and sugar, stirring, to mix it well; put it back on the fire, for about three minutes, stirring slowly, and the same way all the time; when it is thick and well mixed, it is done; take it off immediately, stirring for some time after it is taken off, and flavor with rose-water, or peach-water, to the taste; or instead of cinnamon and rose water, put part of a vanilla bean in a little muslin bag, and boil it in the milk; put it in a dish and grate nutmeg over it.

When you wish it flavored with coffee, you must have some very strong coffee prepared, and add it to the custard, at the same time that you mix the milk and eggs, as otherwise it will be thin. You must flavor it to your taste. Six eggs will be better for coffee custard. If there is a drop of water in the milk it will curdle.

RICE CUSTARD.

Mix a pint of milk, half a pint of cream, one ounce

of rice flour, half dozen bitter almonds, blanched and pounded, with two table-spoonfuls of rose-water; sweeten with loaf sugar, and stir it over the fire till it nearly boils; then add the well beaten yolks of three eggs; let it simmer for about one minute, stirring all the time ; pour it into a dish, or cups, with sugar and nutmeg over it.

SOLID CUSTARD.

One pint of cream, one pint of milk, twenty-one bitter almonds, pounded ; boil together about a quarter of an hour, or until the flavor of the almonds is sufficiently extracted, then set it away to cool ; beat twelve eggs light, leaving out eight whites. When the milk is lukewarm, stir in the eggs, sweeten to your taste, and strain it ; then pour it into a pitcher, and stand it in a vessel of boiling water, and put that on the fire, stirring constantly until it thickens ; then pour it into a dish or cups, and grate nutmeg over it. If you wish to have the custard baked, do not pour it into a pitcher, but put it at once into a dish or cups, and bake in a moderate oven.

ALMOND CUSTARDS.

One pint of cream, quarter of a pound of almonds, blanched and pounded fine, with two table-spoonfuls of rose-water; sweeten to your taste ; beat up the yolks of four eggs; stir all these ingredients together over the fire until the mixture is thick ; then pour it into cups.

JAUNE MANGE, OR HARD CUSTARD.

To a quart of milk, add three pieces of gelatine, (in summer four); after having been well soaked, rub up well the yolks of six eggs, with a quarter of a pound of sugar; melt the gelatine in the milk, and strain it; make the mixture boiling hot, and pour it on the eggs and sugar; let it thicken as you would for custard, and when cool, flavor to your taste, and pour into a mould.

The Russian isinglass is thought preferable, by some persons, to the gelatine.

BLANCMANGE.

One quart of milk, one ounce of isinglass, one dozen bitter almonds, a stick of cinnamon, and a blade or two of mace; dissolve the isinglass in half a pint of water, and mix it with the milk; sweeten to the taste; add the spice and almonds, which must be blanched and broken in a mortar first; then put the saucepan on the fire; let the milk boil five minutes, take it off, and strain it through a towel; stir it until almost cold, then add a tea-cup of Madeira wine, and if the flavor of the almond is not strong enough, add a little peach water; when it begins to thicken, pour it into moulds, which must be first dipped in cold water, and set it away in a cool place to stiffen.

BLANCMANGE MADE WITH GELATINE.

A quart of milk, four pieces of gelatine—soak the gelatine in water, add it to the milk, and let it boil for

five minutes ; strain it through a towel ; sweeten and
flavor to your taste. Coffee blancmange is made by
flavoring it with strong coffee. The shapes should
have cold water put in them, and shaken all round to
prevent the milk from sticking to the sides.

ARROW ROOT BLANCMANGE.

Mix a heaped table-spoonful of arrow root in a little
water ; boil a pint of milk, sweetened and flavored
with a tea-spoonful of rose-water, and half a tea-spoonful of peach-water ; pour it, boiling, on the arrow root ;
boil it again, stirring all the time.

RICE BLANCMANGE. No. 1.

One pint and a half of milk, half a pint of rice flour,
half a pint of white sugar, three dessert-spoonfuls of
rose or peach-water, six of wine or brandy, and a
little spice ; dissolve the sugar in the milk ; add the
spice, and set it to boil. As soon as it boils, add the
rice flour, which must be previously mixed in a half
pint of milk ; stir it frequently while boiling ; when
nearly done, add the essence and liquor. Twenty
minutes are sufficient to boil it, after the flour is mixed
in. While still warm, pour it into a mould, and let
it stand till perfectly congealed.

RICE BLANCMANGE. No. 2.

Boil the rice very tender, and pass it through a
sieve ; sweeten with loaf sugar ; blanch some almonds,

and pound them very fine, adding gradually a little rose or peach-water ; mix all together, and put it into moulds while hot ; make a thin custard, and pour over the blancmange.

RICE FLUMMERY.

Boil six ounces of rice flour slowly, in a quart of milk ; add a little lemon peel, twenty bitter almonds, chopped very fine, and about a quarter of a pound of loaf sugar ; stir it all the time it is on the fire, and when almost boiled to a consistency, pour it into a mould, and let it stand all night, or until it becomes stiff enough to turn out. Serve up with cream and preserves.

CALVES' FEET JELLY.

To a set of feet, allow a gallon and a half of water ; boil slowly till it jellies, skimming the fat off well ; pour it out and let it cool ; when quite stiff, scrape the top carefully, to remove all grease, and put the jelly into a preserving kettle, with sugar enough to sweeten it, the juice of an orange (sour) or lemon, a pint of Teneriffe wine, a gill of brandy, a little cinnamon and lemon, or sweet orange-peel, and the whites and shells of four eggs to clarify it. Let these ingredients boil together until the egg curdles, then strain through a woollen bag until clear.

TO MAKE JELLY.

Soak for two hours in cold water two ounces of

isinglass ; drain off that water, and add two quarts of fresh ; a pound and a half of loaf sugar, the beaten whites of three eggs, the juice of three lemons, the peel of one, and spice to your taste ; stir the whole well together, and boil it five minutes ; strain through a jelly-bag, as often as may be necessary to render it perfectly clear ; pour into moulds, previously moistened with white of egg and water, and set it aside to cool.

For wine jelly, add one pint of wine to the above.

JELLY MADE WITH GELATINE.

A quart of wine, three pints of water, a pound of sugar, two table-spoonfuls of lemon juice, a wineglass of brandy, a stick of cinnamon, eight pieces of gelatine, which should be well soaked in water first ; the whites of eight eggs, slightly beaten ; stir all these together, and put them on the fire ; stir until very hot ; then leave off stirring, and when it boils, let it remain on for five minutes ; take it from the fire, and after it has cooled two minutes, strain it through folded linen or woollen ; continue to pour back until it is quite clear.

RUSSIAN JELLY.

Melt slowly by the fire some seasoned and clarified calves-foot jelly ; when melted, put it into a pan, over ice, and beat it with a whisk as you would floating island ; while beating, squeeze into it, gradually, the juice of a lemon, which will make it perfectly white and light, like floating island. When in this state, put it into a mould or ice, until wanted ; turn it out as you would blancmange or jelly.

Broken bits of jelly, not fit to be brought again to table, will in this manner make a beautiful dish. A good sized tea-cup and a half will fill a large mould, so much does its lightness increase its bulk.

POMONA JELLY

Peel, core and cut into quarters, six large green apples ; throw them into cold water for a few minutes ; then take them out, and add about five ounces of powdered loaf sugar ; stew them till quite soft ; rub them through a sieve, and add three-quarters of an ounce of isinglass, which must be first dissolved in about a half pint of water. Rub some sugar upon the peel of a lemon, to extract the flavor ; add it to the jelly, and if not sweet enough, add more sugar ; stir it over the fire till quite hot ; then put it into a mould, and turn out the next day.

ORANGE JELLY.

The juice of eight oranges, and six lemons ; grate the peel of half the fruit, and steep it in a pint of cold water ; when the flavor is extracted, mix the water with the juice ; add three quarters of a pound of loaf sugar, one and a quarter ounces of isinglass, and the beaten whites of seven eggs ; put all into a saucepan, and stir till it boils. Let it boil a few minutes ; strain it, till clear, through a jelly-bag ; put it into a mould, or glasses.

———+— -

BAVARIAN CREAM.

Two ounces of best Russian isinglass boiled in two quarts of water till reduced to one ; strain it while warm, and add to it one and a half pounds of powdered sugar ; put it into a deep vessel to cool ; whip up two quarts of thick cream to a stiff froth, which, as it forms, take off with a spoon, and lay upon a sieve to drain, so that none but the solid part is retained. When the cream is all frothed, add to it the melted isinglass and sugar, into which the flavoring substance must be previously put. When it is all mixed together, put it into moulds and set it on ice. In about an hour it will be stiff enough to turn out. When to be flavored with vanilla, break up two fresh beans in a pint of water, and simmer down to half the quantity in a covered vessel ; strain it, and mix it with the isinglass and sugar, before they are added to the cream.

—— +·—

A SIMILAR DISH, MORE SIMPLE AND ECONOMICAL.

Half a pint of milk, six eggs, six ounces of sugar ; flavor with vanilla, or any other essence. Beat till very light, and let it simmer on the fire (without boiling) for fifteen minutes. When it becomes tepid, mix

13

in half a pint of whipped cream ; pour it into a mould, and surround it with ice.   Whip up some cream, and pour it into the dish after the form is turned out.

———•———

BURNT CREAM.

Put a boiled custard in a dish ; when cold, grate sugar over it, and brown it with a salamander or a hot shovel.

———•———

COFFEE CREAM.

Put a quart of water into a coffee-pot ; when it boils, put in two ounces of coffee ; stir well, and let it boil up two or three times ; let it stand till you can draw it off clear, then pour into a stew-pan, with one pint of milk, well sweetened ; let it boil away till there is only enough left to fill your dessert-dish ; rub into it the yolks of five eggs, a tea-spoonful of flour, and half a pint of cream ; let the dish be then placed in a stew-pan of water just ready to boil, place it on the fire, and let it boil only till the cream becomes smooth. —*Madame de Genlis.*

———•———

RATAFIA CREAM.

Break five eggs, and beat up the yolks with some cream and a large spoonful of finely powdered sugar ; put into a saucepan a quart of thick cream and six laurel-leaves, or a few bitter almonds, and set it on the fire. When it has once boiled up, throw away the leaves and put in the beaten eggs ; stir all together,

and keep it hot for some time, without allowing it to
boil, observing to stir always the same way.   When
thick enough, pour it into cups for the table.

STRAWBERRY CREAM.

Boil a pint of milk, well sweetened, and moisten a
dessert-spoonful of flour with a little of the hot milk ;
throw it into the milk on the fire, and stir with a
wooden spoon ; pour in the juice of crushed strawberries till the cream becomes of the color you want, and
strain the whole through a sieve.

ORANGE CREAM.

The juice of four sour oranges, and the peel of one,
chipped fine ; put them into a stew-pan, with half a
pint of water and half a pound of loaf sugar ; beat the
whites of five eggs, and add them ; set the pan over a
slow fire ; stir one way until it grows thick and white ;
then strain through a bit of muslin, and stir till cold.
Beat the yolks of five eggs very light, and put them
into your pan with the cream ; stir over a slow fire till
ready to boil ; pour it into a bowl, and stir till cold ;
then put it into your glasses.

ALMOND CREAM.

Boil a quart of cream with a grated nutmeg, a blade
or two of mace, a bit of lemon-peel, and sugar to the
taste.   Blanch a quarter of a pound of almonds, and

beat them very fine with a dessert-spoonful of rose (or orange-flower) water. Beat well the whites of nine eggs, strain and add them to the almonds; beat them together, rub them through a coarse hair sieve, and mix all together with the cream; set it on the fire, stir it one way until it almost boils; then pour it into a bowl and stir till cold; then put it into cups or glasses.

LEMON CREAM.

Take five large lemons, pare them as thin as possible, and steep the parings with the juice of the lemons in twenty spoonfuls of spring-water; then strain into a silver saucepan through a jelly-bag, and add the whites (well beaten) of six eggs, and ten ounces of loaf sugar; set the saucepan over a very slow fire, stirring all the time one way; skim it, and when hot, pour it into glasses, slowly.

SNOW CREAM.

Put some thin slices of sponge-cake in the bottom of a dish; pour in wine enough to soak it. Beat up the whites of three eggs *very* hard; add to it two table-spoonfuls of finely powdered sugar, a glass of sweet wine, and a pint of rich cream. Beat these well in, and pour over the cake.

CURD AND CREAM.

Take a pint of fresh milk; mix with it a glass of sweet cream; turn it with rennet. When turned, put it in a curd-press, and let it drain for some hours. When the cheese is well drained, turn it out in a deep dish two-thirds full of good cream. Instead of turning the milk with rennet, clabber may be used in making the curd. Serve with sugar and nutmeg.

SLIP.

Put into a dish a quart of cream and one of milk, and stir into it a table-spoonful and a half of " Artichoke Extract." The length of time required to turn the milk depends upon the weather. In a warm climate it will congeal in three-quarters of an hour, and in a cool one it should be mixed very soon after breakfast, if wanted for dinner. Grate nutmeg and cinnamon over the top, and serve with sugar and cream.

NOTE.—The " Extract" is made by filling a bottle with the dried flowers of the artichoke, and pouring as much wine upon them as the bottle will hold; or in the following manner :—A few hours before it is wanted, put into a table-spoonful and a half of water a dessert-spoonful of the dried flowers. Let them steep, and strain the water into the milk.

TO MAKE SOLID SYLLABUBS.

One pint of cream, half a pint of wine, the juice and grated peel of one lemon, sweetened to your taste ; put it in a wide-mouthed bottle, shake it for ten minutes, then pour it into your glasses. It must be made the evening before it is to be used.

13*

SYLLABUB.

To one quart of cream put half a pint of sweet wine and half a pint of Madeira, the juice of two lemons, a little finely powdered spice, and sugar to the taste. The peel of the lemons must be steeped in the wine until the flavor is extracted. Whisk all these ingredients together, and as the froth rises take it off with a spoon, lay it upon a fine sieve; what drains from it put into your pan again and whisk it. Put the froth into glasses.

TRIFLE.

Lay in the bottom of a glass dish or bowl half a pound of macaroons and a few slices of sponge cake; wet them thoroughly with ratafia or sweet wine. Whisk together the following ingredients: one quart of cream, half a pint of milk, one pint of Teneriffe wine, the grated peel of two lemons and the juice of one, a little finely powdered spice, and sugar to the taste; as the froth rises, take it off and lay it upon the cake until the dish is full.

A custard may be put first upon the cake, and the froth laid lightly upon that.

APPLE FLOAT.

One dozen large green apples, boiled in as little water as possible, and passed through a fine hair sieve; when cold, sweeten to the taste, add the whites of two eggs well beaten, and then beat the whole with a

spoon until it is quite stiff. When ready for the table,
grate nutmeg over it. It must be eaten with cream.

TO MAKE A DISH OF SNOW.

Take eight or nine apples, put them in cold water,
and set them over a slow fire ; when they are soft, put
them upon a hair sieve to drain ; take off the skin, and
put the pulp into a bowl ; then beat the white of three
eggs to a very strong froth ; sweeten it to your taste
with sugar sifted very fine, and strewed into the eggs.
Beat the pulp of your apples also into a stiff froth ;
then beat them together till they resemble snow. Lay
this upon a china dish, and heap it up as high as possible, placing at the top a piece of myrtle, and orna-
menting it round the bottom of the pyramid.

MOCK ICE.

Take about three table-spoonfuls of some good preserve ; rub it through a sieve with as much cream
(say a quart) as will fill a mould. Dissolve three-
fourths of an ounce of isinglass in half a pint of water;
when almost cold, mix it well with the cream, put it
into a mould, set it in a cool place, and turn out the
next day.

BOILED ICING.

One and a half pounds of loaf sugar, boiled in half a
pint of water until it ropes ; beat the whites of seven

eggs to a stiff froth ; put the syrup into a boil, and stir
it until it is milk warm ; then put in the eggs, and
beat the whole one hour.

ICES.

ALMOND ICE.

Two pints of milk, eight ounces of cream, two ounces of orange-flower water, eight ounces of sweet almonds, four ounces of bitter almonds, twelve ounces of sugar; blanch the almonds, and pound in a marble mortar, pouring in, from time to time, a few drops of water; when thoroughly pounded, add the orange-flower water and half the milk; pass this, tightly squeezed, through a cloth. Boil the rest of the milk with the cream, and keep stirring it with a wooden spoon; as soon as it is thick enough, pour in the almond milk; give it one boiling; take it off and let it cool in a bowl or pitcher before pouring it into the mould for freezing.—*Madame de Genlis.*

VANILLA ICE.

Two pints of milk, eight ounces of cream, four grains of vanilla, twelve ounces of sugar; split the vanilla, and cut it into small pieces; beat it with a little sugar in a marble mortar till it becomes powdered; put it into a stew-pan or skillet, with the milk, cream and sugar; let them boil till the whole is sufficiently thick, then strain through a cloth, and pour into a bowl to cool.—*Madame de Genlis.*

CHOCOLATE ICE.

Have six yolks of eggs and three-fourths of a pound of sugar well stirred together, as if for cake ; roll out a quarter of a pound of chocolate, pour a tea-cupful of boiling water on it, a little at a time, until it is well mixed ; boil a quart of cream and one of milk toge-ther ; when it boils, mix it with the chocolate, a little at a time ; then put it on the fire, and when it boils, pour it on the eggs, mixing it all the time ; put it again on the fire, and stir it until it becomes thick : it must not boil. When cold, freeze it.

MILK ICE. No. 1.

Take the quantity of milk you wish frozen, sweeten and flavor with rose-water or peach-water, or any-thing you please ; freeze it. This is much better than cream in summer. Boiling the milk makes some dif-ference in the flavor, and is preferred by some people.

MILK ICE. No. 2.

To two quarts of milk allow four pieces of gelatine ; soak the gelatine well in water ; boil it in the milk till it dissolves ; strain and sweeten it ; flavor it with whatever you please.

CUSTARD ICE.

Prepare some good custard ; make it very sweet, and flavor it highly ; put in as much cream as you have custard, and freeze.

MATRIMONY.

Pare and cut in small pieces two dozen common sized peaches; cover them thickly with sugar, and let them stand three or four hours; beat them into a quart of cream, or a very rich custard—(if cream, sweeten); freeze.

ROMAN PUNCH.

Make a rich lemonade (of limes, if they can be had), and to two quarts of the lemonade allow half a pint of old rum and half a pint of peach brandy; stir all well together, and freeze.

STRAWBERRY SHERBET.

Three pounds of strawberries, eight ounces of red currants, one pint of water; crush the strawberries and currants in a sieve, and let the juice run into a deep dish or bowl; pour the water over the strawberries remaining in the sieve; melt the sugar in a little water over the fire, and add to the juice, and pour it into the mould.

LEMON SHERBET.

Make any quantity you please of good lemonade (it is better made of limes); make it very sweet, and freeze it.

PINE-APPLE SHERBET. No. 1.

Take two or three very ripe pine-apples; pare them

and grate them into a bowl; put the grated pine-apple on a sieve, and let it drain well, pressing it down, to get out every drop of the juice. Weaken it as much as you please with water, and make it very sweet, as all things, when frozen, have less flavor.

PINE-APPLE SHERBET. No. 2.

Extract the juice from two ripe pine-apples and one lemon; add a pound and a half of white sugar; then pour on three quarts of boiling water; stir well, and strain through a sieve or coarse towel; then freeze it.

PEACH SHERBET.

Get two or three dozen ripe, soft, freestone peaches; peal them and pass them through a colander; add water sufficient to weaken it, and sweeten to the taste; freeze.

BLACKBERRY SHERBET.

The juice extracted from six quarts of blackberries, strained and sweetened, will make two quarts of sherbet. A pint of milk added, is thought by some persons an improvement.

PRESERVES, ETC.

WHITE COMPOTE OF PEARS.

BLANCH as many pears as you intend to use, whole, with the skin on, in boiling water; take them out when soft, peel, and put into cold water. Have your syrup ready in the stew-pan; when it is boiling hot, put in the pears, with a slice of lemon to keep them white; when thoroughly stewed, take them out, and serve in the syrup. They may be served hot or cold. Red compote of pears is made as above, only leave out the lemon, and cover the stew-pan with a pewter plate: but this red color is only given by the pewter to fruit preserved in a bell-metal vessel.

COMPOTE OF STRAWBERRIES.

Boil half a pound of sugar with half a pint of water till it becomes a very thick syrup. Take care to skim it well. Have ready your strawberries, well picked, washed and drained, and not over ripe; put them into the syrup; take them off, after being a minute or two on the fire, to let them settle; put them back, let them boil once, and take off quickly.

Raspberry compote is made in the same manner, but the raspberries must not be washed.

14

COMPOTE OF PEACHES.

Blanch your peaches in boiling water; when quite soft, take them out with a strainer, put them into cold water; have ready in your stew-pan a syrup made of a quarter of a pound of sugar and half a pint of water; put in your peaches, let them boil two or three times, skim them well, place in a dessert-dish, and pour the syrup over them.

Apricots are stewed in the same manner.

WHITE COMPOTE OF APPLES.

Cut six large apples in half; peel and take out the seeds; stew them in a pint of water, the juice of half a lemon, and sugar. When the apples are sufficiently tender, take them out and arrange them in the dessert-dish. Let the syrup keep on boiling till it is clear and rich, then pour it over the apples.—*Madame de Genlis*.

PEACH MARMALADE.

Take very ripe peaches, peel them, take out the stones, and cover them with all the sugar you mean to use for them. A pound of sugar to a pound of fruit is enough to make very nice marmalade; but if you wish the flavor of the fruit to be very well preserved, take a pound and a half of sugar to the pound. After the peaches have been in the sugar three or four hours, turn them into your preserving-kettle, boil them very rapidly half an hour, if you use a pound, and eight or ten minutes, if you have a pound and a half. Rub it with a spoon through a hair sieve, and fill your jars immediately. Made thus, this marmalade has the transparency of jelly.

PEACH LEATHER.

Take a peck or two of soft freestone peaches, pound them, pass the pulp through a coarse sieve, and to four quarts of pulp add one quart of good brown sugar; mix them well together, and boil for about two minutes; spread the paste on plates, and put them in the sun every day until the cakes look dry, and will leave the plates readily by passing a knife round the edges of the cakes; dust some sugar over the rough side, and roll them up like sweet wafers. If kept in a dry place they will continue sound for some months. If the weather is fine, three days will be enough to dry them.

TO DRY PEACHES.

Take nearly ripe peaches, and separate them from the stones in as large pieces as possible; then take their weight of sugar; to every pound of sugar add half a pint of water; boil it into a syrup, taking off the scum as it rises; when the syrup is cold, pour it over the peaches, and set them to boil in an open skillet; let them boil slowly until they are very tender, then take them from the syrup with a fish-knife, and lay them in flat dishes to dry in the sun; put them out every day, and now and then turn them; if the weather be damp or rainy, put them in a warm oven; when nearly dry, throw the syrup over them, first boiling it almost to a candy, and then renew the above directed process for drying.

N. B.—To make peach cake, boil the peaches to a jelly, and dry it in earthen dishes.

—————

TO PRESERVE PEACHES.

Gather your peaches full grown, but not ripe enough for eating; allow three-fourths of a pound of sugar to every pound of fruit; pare and put them into a bowl, sprinkling sugar between each layer; let them lie twelve hours, in which time the juice will be drawn; then put them into the preserving-kettle, and boil until transparent. Before putting the peaches into the kettle, pour in a glass of brandy.

—————

TO PRESERVE PEACHES FOR TARTS.

Gather your peaches in any state not under half ripe; pare, and put them into a jar with an equal weight of sugar, sprinkled among them; put them into the oven, and bake them.

—————

MARMALADE.

Peel and cut up small, six pounds of peaches or apricots, crack the stones, blanch the kernels, and mince them up extremely fine; add six pounds of

sugar, and put all together into your preserving-kettle;
set it on a slow fire, keep stirring it, and mash the
pieces smooth; when sufficiently boiled and thick,
take it off and put it away for winter tarts. If preserved for immediate use, four and a half pounds of
sugar.

TO PRESERVE SHADDOCKS.

Prepare the fruit by carving or grating off the outer
rind; keep them in salt and water till all are ready;
then boil them well in soft water, changing the water
as soon as it becomes bitter; for this purpose keep a
kettle of warm water ready, as cold water poured over
them would make them hard; when sufficiently tender
and sweet, put the shaddocks into a good syrup, and
boil them until they become transparent; for the
syrup, allow one and a half pounds of loaf sugar to
every pound of fruit.

N. B. After the shaddocks are boiled, a small piece
should be cut from the stem end, and the tough strings
in the centre extracted with a pen knife, before they
are put into the syrup.

SOUR ORANGE MARMALADE.

Weigh your fruit, and allow one and a half pounds
loaf sugar to one pound oranges; cut them in half;
squeeze the juice through a sieve, upon the sugar;
pick out the pulp from the skins and seeds, and add
i t to the juice; put the seeds into a bowl, and cover
14*

them with cold water; when the jelly has formed
around them, put them upon a sieve, and press the
jelly through it; add it to the juice and pulp; boil
the skins until they become quite tender, changing the
water until the bitter is sufficiently extracted; take
them out of the kettle, and drain the water from them;
scoop out the pith, and pound the skins in a marble
mortar until quite fine; mix it with the juice, &c., &c.,
and boil for an hour, stirring frequently. Some persons reserve one-third of the skins to cut into strips,
which are boiled with the juice, &c.

TO PRESERVE ORANGES.

Grate your oranges lightly, so as just to break the
skin, that the oil may be extracted in boiling; then
cut them in quarters, or any shape you please, squeeze
them and take out the pulp; then boil the skins till
they are tender, observing to change the water two or
three times while boiling, and taking care to use *boiling* water only, in making these changes; when done,
spread them in a dish to drain: then weigh them,
and to one pound of skins, put two pounds of sugar.
The syrup must be made thin, a quart of water to one
pound of sugar, to allow the skins to boil until they
are perfectly clear.

TO PRESERVE YELLOW ORANGES.

Grate or peel off the glazed skin of the oranges,
then cut them in half and squeeze the juice; pour a
little boiling water on the seeds, which, when cold, will

form a jelly ; boil the peels, changing the water five
or six times, until the bitterness is sufficiently extracted, and they are tender ; then throw them in cold
water, and let them remain until the next day. After
removing the pulp, weigh the peels, then cover them
in clean cold water, there to remain until the syrup is
boiled ; make the syrup with the jelly strained from
the seeds, the juice and an equal quantity of sugar to
the weight of the oranges, boil till clear, then drain
the peels from the water, and throw them into the
boiling syrup ; continue the boiling until the peels are
transparent.

TO CANDY ORANGE PEEL.

Leave your oranges on the tree until the rind is
thick—any time in January will do. Weigh the fruit,
and allow an equal weight of sugar ; cut the oranges
in half, and take out the pulp ; boil the peels until
quite tender, changing the water (which should be
hot,) frequently ; cover the kettle close while the peels
are boiling ; moisten your sugar, put in the peels, and
boil them until thoroughly impregnated with the syrup ;
then take out the peels, lay them on tin sheets, and
put them in a cool oven. When quite dry, lay them
again in the syrup until they become saturated , return
them to the oven, and continue the process until the
syrup is exhausted.

ORANGE WAFERS

Take the best oranges, cut them in half, and take

out the seeds and juice : boil them in three or four
waters till they are tender, then beat them to pulp in a
marble mortar, and rub them through a hair sieve ; to
one pound of this pulp, allow a pound and a half of
loaf sugar; take half of your sugar, and boil it with
the oranges till it becomes ropy ; then take it from the
fire, and when cold, make it up in paste with the
other half of your sugar ; make but a little at a time,
for it will dry fast ; then with a rolling pin, roll them
out as thin as tiffany, upon paper. Cut them round
with a wine-glass, let them dry, and they will look
clear.

TO PRESERVE FIGS.

Pick your figs when a little more than half ripe ;
peel them very thin, and to a pound of fruit put three-
quarters of a pound of sugar ; make a syrup, and put
the figs into it, with a good deal of stick cinnamon ;
let them boil till clear, stirring frequently.

TO MAKE TOMATO PRESERVES.

Take the tomatoes while small and green ; put them
in cold clarified syrup, with one orange cut in slices,
to every two pounds of tomatoes ; but if very superior
preserves are wanted, add instead of the orange, two
fresh lemons, to three pounds of tomatoes ; simmer
them over a slow fire for two or three hours.

TO PRESERVE CHERRIES.

Wash your cherries, and prick each one with a large

needle; to each pound of cherries allow one pound of loaf sugar; break your sugar into large lumps, and dip them into water; put them into your kettle, and when the syrup begins to boil, throw in the cherries; let them remain until you can see the stones, then take them out and spread them upon a dish; let the syrup continue to boil until perfectly clear; the next day put the cherries into the syrup. The juice which has drained from the fruit must not be added to the syrup. This makes a very pretty sweetmeat when preserved with the stems.

PUMPKIN CHIPS.

Cut slices from a high-colored pumpkin, and cut the slices into chips about the thickness of a dollar; wash them, dry them thoroughly, and weigh them against an equal weight of sugar; add to each pound of sugar half a pint of lime or lemon-juice; boil and skim it, then add the pumpkin; when half boiled, take the slices out of the syrup and let them cool; then return them, and boil until the pumpkin becomes clear. The peel of the lemons or limes, pared very thin, boiled until tender, and added to the chips when nearly done, is an improvement.

TO BRANDY THE AUGUST PLUM.

Select the largest and ripest plums, prick each one with a silver fork, put them into a glass jar, and cover them with brandy; let them steep ten days or a fortnight; then take them out of the brandy, weigh them, and to each pound of plums allow three quarters of a pound of white sugar; let the plums lie on the sugar until it becomes saturated, then put it all into your kettle, and boil about half an hour over a slow fire.

The brandy in which the plums have been steeped makes a delightful cordial when sweetened, and a few cloves and a little cinnamon added.

QUINCE MARMALADE.

Weigh equal quantities of quinces and sugar; wet the sugar sufficiently with white of egg to clarify it; scald the quinces until the skins crack; when cold, the skins can be easily taken off with the fingers; then scrape off all the soft part of the fruit with a spoon, put it to the syrup, and boil till perfectly clear. Put it up in shallow boxes.

QUINCE JELLY.

Cut your quinces into quarters, and cut out the defective parts, but do not pare or core them; cover them with soft water, and boil them until very tender. When done, strain them through a coarse cloth, and to every pint of juice allow a pound of loaf sugar. Boil until the jelly is well formed.

BRANDY SWEETMEATS.

To three pounds of sugar add a pint and a half of

water; boil and skim it; prepare eight pounds of ripe clingstone peaches, washed and rubbed with a coarse towel until all the down is off; then pierce them well with a fork, throw them into the syrup, and boil them until a sharp straw can penetrate them; as they soften, put them into your jar, which must be kept closely covered; boil your syrup until it thickens, and while hot add a quart of best brandy, and throw it over your peaches; tie the jar down closely.

PINE-APPLE SWEETMEATS.

Grate two or three very ripe pine-apples; put a pound of sugar to a pint of grated fruit; let it boil up for twenty minutes. If properly done, the sweetmeat will look like threads of gold.

APPLE JELLY.

Chop into small pieces twelve common sized tart apples; cover them with water, and let them boil till soft; then run them through a colander, and with a spoon press out as much of the substance as possible, and if not too thick pass it through a flannel bag; if it should be too thick, add more water to the peel and cores of the apples; boil them, and add the juice to the pulp. After it has been passed through the flannel bag, put a pound of sugar to a quart of the pulp, and set it to boil; when it becomes clear, and a jelly forms round the kettle, it is done.

Take the pulp of the apples remaining in the bag, and to one pound of this pulp allow one pound of loaf sugar. This, when boiled, makes a nice marmalade.

Three or four guavas, cut up and put with the apples when first set to boil, makes very good jelly and marmalade. If none of the guava can be procured, lemon-peel may be used to flavor it.

TOMATO JELLY.

Fill a large jar with slices of the ripest and best tomatoes; lay a cloth over the jar, and over that put a piece of dough, to keep in the heat; place the jar in a large pot of water, and boil four or five hours, constantly; then strain the juice through a coarse hair sieve, and to every pint of juice put a pound of brown sugar, if you wish the jelly very sweet, or half that quantity if to eat with meat. Add the whites of eight eggs to every gallon of juice, skim it, and boil till nearly half evaporated; then put it in glasses, and keep them in the sun till sufficiently thick.

A very good jelly to eat with meat may be made by putting salt, pepper, and a little mace and nutmeg instead of sugar.

SAGO JELLY.

One pint of the juice of any fruit mixed with a pint of water, half a pint of sago, some cinnamon, one lemon (juice and peel), and four small cups of sugar. The jelly made in the usual way.

LIQUEURS, SYRUPS, ETC.

Two ounces of cinnamon; one of cloves, mace and nutmeg each; one-fourth of a pound of allspice. Bruise your spice pretty fine, and put it into a jug with a gallon of water; stew it till you judge the strength of the spice is extracted; then strain the water through a flannel bag, add the rest of the allspice (only one-fourth of the quantity above mentioned being at first put into the water), and two gallons of wine. Sweeten to your taste, cork it lightly, let it just boil, and strain it again.

GINGER WINE.

Boil fifteen pounds of loaf sugar in eight gallons of water; skim it clear; then let it stand until it is cold. Bruise one and a half pounds of the best ginger, the rinds of six lemons (which, with the ginger, must be boiled in three pints of water for an hour). When cold, add the juice, half a pound of raisins (split), and three table-spoonfuls of yeast. Set it to ferment one day and night before putting it in stone bottles—tie down the cork.

ELDER WINE.

To every quart of elder-berries add a quart of water, the berries having been kept three or four days after

15

being gathered ; boil them for half an hour longer, with three pounds of sugar, two and a half ounces of ginger, one ounce of allspice and a few cloves, to a gallon. All the spices must be half bruised. When nearly cold, add a piece of bread dipped in yeast, to ferment it.

RASPBERRY WINE.

Take fourteen quarts of raspberries, bruise them well, and put them into fourteen pints of spring water ; let it stand twenty-four hours, then strain it off ; take fourteen pounds of moist sugar, with four quarts of water and the whites of four eggs, just make it boil up, and skim it well ; let it stand till it is almost cold, then mix it with the juice, put it into a barrel, and let it stand eight days to ferment ; then take two quarts of brandy, and one drachm of cochineal, pounded very fine, put it into the barrel, stop it close for three months, at which time it will be fit for bottling.— *English Receipt.*

EGG WINE.

The yolks of three eggs must be well beaten with a table-spoonful of cold water ; take then half a pint of white wine, with the same quantity of cold water, sweeten it to your taste, and make it boil up ; then put a small quantity to the egg, and beat them well together ; after that is done, throw the egg and the negus from bowl to bowl until it is thoroughly mixed. It must be about the consistency of thin chocolate, and must froth,

EGG NOGG.

Six eggs, a quart of milk, half a pint of brandy, six
table-spoonfuls of sugar; beat the yolks and sugar together, and the whites very hard; mix in the brandy;
boil the milk and pour it into the mixture.

SHERRY COBBLER.

Fill a tumbler half full of crushed ice, having first
put in the tumbler a table-spoonful and a half of powdered sugar and a slice or two of lemon; pour on
it a wineglassful of sherry wine; pour from tumbler
to tumbler till it is well mixed.

QUINCE CORDIAL.

Take ripe quinces, pare and rasp them, strain the
juice through a linen cloth; to ten pints add eight of
good brandy. Then take two pounds and a half of
loaf sugar, eight ounces of bitter almonds, one ounce
of coriander seed, and half an ounce of cloves; mix
and bruise them all together, and put them in a china
or earthen vessel, closely covered. Shake it every
day for ten days; then run it off through a jelly-bag
until it is quite clear.

Peach-kernels will do instead of bitter almonds.

ORANGE CORDIAL.

Pare fourteen oranges and fourteen lemons very thin;

put to the peel five quarts of brandy, and let it stand twelve hours; squeeze the juice of the oranges and lemons on five pounds of loaf sugar; the next day add five quarts of cold water and two of boiling milk; stir all the ingredients well together, and let the mixture stand twelve hours; then run it through a flannel bag, and it is fit for use. Bottle it close.

GOLDEN CORDIAL.

To one gallon of brandy add the rinds of four or six lemons, according to their size; expose this to the sun eight or ten days, shaking it once every day; then strain the brandy from the rinds, and add two pounds of loaf sugar, one ounce of almonds, one ounce of peach-kernels, one ounce of cinnamon, and twenty-five cloves. Let these steep in the brandy until the flavor is extracted, then filter for use.

RATAFIA.

Steep for several months in a gallon of brandy twelve hundred peach-kernels (blanched). When the flavor is extracted from the kernels, pour off the brandy, and add to it one quart of Frontignac wine, one quart of strong hyson tea, one pint of orange-flower water, and three pounds of white sugar; stir all well together, and bottle it. As soon as it becomes clear it may be used, but improves with age.

SIMPLE MADE (IMITATION) ORGEAT.

A pint of water to two pounds of white sugar, boiled for five minutes; when cold, add a table-spoonful of essence of bitter almonds, and a table-spoonful of essence of rose, or a few large spoonfuls of good rose-water; mix the whole well together, and bottle.

SIROP D'ORGEAT.

Take half a pound of sweet almonds, two ounces of bitter almonds, a pint and three-quarters of water, two pounds and a half of sugar, two ounces orange-flower water, two drachms of essence of lemon; beat in a mortar the almonds, pouring in little by little some of the water to keep them from oiling; when they are reduced to a paste, add the rest of the water; mix it well together, and pass it through a sieve.; melt the sugar in the emulsion, and after it becomes cold, add the orange-flower water and essence of lemon. Almonds are bleached by pouring boiling water on them.—*French Receipt.*

ORANGE-FLOWER SYRUP.

To a quarter of a pound of dried blossoms, add two pounds of sugar, and four pints of water; boil to a rich syrup.

N. B. The orange-blossoms should be gathered as soon as they fall from the tree, however few in num-

15*

ber ; keep them in a cool shady place till a sufficient quantity be procured for boiling.

———◆———

RASPBERRY VINEGAR.

On two quarts of fresh raspberries, pour one pint of white wine vinegar. The next day put the fruit into a linen bag, and press out all the juice, and pour it on two more quarts of fresh raspberries ; express the juice as before ; repeat this four or five times ; then strain the liquor, and to every pint of juice allow one pound of loaf sugar ; put it all into a stone jar, in a pot of hot water, over the fire ; let the water boil well for an hour, and after it has stood about half an hour, there will be a scum on the vinegar ; take the jar out of the water, and let it stand till perfectly cold ; then take off the scum, and bottle it for use.

———◆———

SIROP DE VINAIGRE FRAMBOISE.

Steep two pounds of raspberries in a pint and a half of good undistilled vinegar for four days ; pour it off without squeezing them ; clarify four pounds of sugar in a pint and a half of water, and add it to the flavored vinegar ; add also four ounces of brandy.

———◆———

LIME SYRUP

Squeeze your limes, and strain the juice into a vessel large enough to hold all the ingredients. To one quart of juice add three and a half pounds of loaf sugar, and let it remain all night; the next morning there will be a scum, which must be removed with a spoon. Strain the syrup, and bottle it for use.

LEMONADE.

To one quart of lemon juice, add three pounds of powdered loaf sugar; allow the scum to rise one night, then skim.

REGENT'S PUNCH.

To two quarts of green tea, add half a pint of currant jelly, a little champagne, and the juice of four lemons; sweeten with loaf sugar, and add old spirits or brandy to your taste.

IMPERIAL.

Pare your limes *very thin;* fill the bottle with the peel; then cover it with brandy, and let it steep until the flavor is extracted from the peel—a week or ten days. On a table-spoonful of cream of tartar, pour four quarts of boiling water, and add three large table-spoonfuls of the lime brandy. Sweeten to your taste, stir well, and set it in ice to cool.

IRISH MEAD.

Five gallons of water, two and a half pints of honey, one pound of raisins (stoned), half a pound of currants, three ounces of eringo-root (not candied), one ounce of liquorice, one ounce of China-root, quarter of an ounce of coriander seed, two sprigs of rosemary; boil all these in the water until reduced to four gallons; then strain, and when cool work it up with yeast as in making ale; put it into another vessel, let it stand seven days, and then bottle it. As soon as brisk it is fit for use.

PEA-HAULM BEER.

Pour six gallons of water on one bushel of the shells of green peas, and boil till the shells become tasteless; then pour off the water into a clean tub or keg, and add to it one pint of yeast, and two ounces of powdered ginger. In a short time fermentation will begin, and when it is complete, the beer will be fit for use.

Beer made thus, is very clear, has a fine amber color, is pungent to the taste, and bears a fine head—far superior to the common molasses beer, and not inferior to mead.

One bushel of the shells (or haulms), will make several dozen bottles of beer. It should be put into strong bottles, the corks secured with wire, and kept in a cool cellar.

SPRUCE BEER.

One pint of sassafras root (in chips), one handful of the tender tops of the spruce pine, one quart of molasses, two gallons of water. Put these ingredients together into a jug, cork it tight, shake it well, and let it stand twenty-four hours ; then bottle it, cork tightly, and in twelve hours it will be fit for use.

When the jug used is new, two table-spoonfuls of rough rice and two of corn must be added to the other ingredients, in order to hasten the ripening of the beer.

PINE-APPLE BEER.

Wash and then pare a pine-apple ; if a good size, put the rind into about two quarts of water (in the quantity you must be guided by the size of the pine-apple) ; cover it for twenty-four hours ; then sweeten to your taste, bottle, cork, and put it into the sun for five or six hours, cool it, and it is then fit for use.

GINGER BEER.

Three lemons, two ounces of ginger, two ounces of cream of tartar, two and a half pounds of white sugar ; two gallons of boiling water poured on the above ingredients, and when milk warm, add two table-spoonfuls of yeast. The whole, when cold, to be strained through a thick towel, so as to take out all kinds of sediment, and then put it in stone bottles and tie down the cork.

PICKLES, ETC.

TO MAKE ATZJAR.

EIGHT ounces of ginger; let it lie in salt and water one night; scrape and cut it into thin slices. One pound of garlic, peeled and cut into small pieces; salt it for three days, then wash and dry it in the sun upon a sieve. Put the ginger and garlic into a jar, with an ounce of turmeric, finely powdered, a quarter of a pound of white mustard seed, washed and bruised, and a gallon of white wine vinegar. The pickle ought to stand a fortnight, or longer, before the vegetables are put into it. Pare the cucumbers, and take out all the seeds; if large, cut them in pieces; salt them for three days, and dry them in the sun, upon a sieve. Cabbages are to be cut into quarters, and salted as the cucumbers; the water must be squeezed out before they are dried. In the same manner do cauliflowers, celery, radishes (scraping the latter), French beans (leaving the young tops on). Asparagus must be salted but two days; give them a boil up in salt and water, then dry them as the others.

You need never empty your jar; but as the season comes on, dry the vegetables and put them in all together, and fill up with vinegar. Be careful no rain or damp comes to them, for that will make them rot.

SPICED PEACHES.

Seven pounds of peaches, pared and cut in half; three pounds of good brown sugar; one quart of vinegar; one tea-spoonful of powdered cloves; one tea-spoonful of powdered cinnamon. Boil the spice, sugar and vinegar together for fifteen minutes; then add the fruit, and boil until soft.

TO PICKLE PEACHES.

Gather your peaches when they are at their full growth, and just before they begin to ripen: be sure they are not bruised. Then take soft water, as much as you think will cover them; make it salt enough to bear an egg, with equal quantities of bay and common salt; then put in your peaches, and put a weight upon them, to keep them under water; let them stand three days; then take them out, wipe them carefully with a soft cloth, and lay them in your jar. Take as much white wine vinegar as will fill your jar, and to every gallon put one pint of the best (well mixed) mustard, two or three heads of garlic, a good deal of green ginger (sliced), half an ounce of cloves, half an ounce of mace, half an ounce of nutmeg. Mix your pickle well together, and pour it over your peaches; put them into jars, and cover them with bladder or leather, carefully tied. They will be fit for use in two months.

The peaches may be cut across, the stones taken out, and their places filled with mustard-seed, garlic, horse-radish and ginger; the pieces are then tied together.

Apricots and nectarines may be pickled in the same way.

TO PICKLE DAMSONS.

Seven pounds of plums, three pounds of sugar, one ounce of cloves, one ounce of cinnamon, one quart of vinegar; put a layer of plums and a layer of spice (not powdered) alternately; boil the sugar and vinegar together, and pour over the fruit; the next day boil up all together, and put away for use.

TO PICKLE MANGOES.

One pound of horse-radish (finely shred) put into a strong salt pickle for twenty-four hours; one pound of garlic and one pound of ginger in a like pickle for three or four weeks, changing the pickle every third day. After the radish, garlic and ginger have been in pickle the time stated, take them out, dry them in the sun, and add one pound of white mustard seed, one pound of white pepper, one-fourth of a pound of turmeric, two ounces each of mace, cloves and nutmegs, and one quart of olive oil; put all into a marble mortar, and pound to a paste; with this paste stuff the mangoes. A bottle of mustard to be made, and mixed with a sufficiency of white wine vinegar to cover the mangoes.

The proportions in this receipt will pickle one hundred mangoes.

16

TO PICKLE BELL-PEPPERS.

Cut holes in the peppers, and if you do not wish them hot, take out the seeds; pour boiling water upon them, and let them remain until the water is cold; then take them out, pack them for twenty-four hours in salt; dry them well, and put them into vinegar. Mustard seed, spices, &c., can be added to your taste.

TO PICKLE RADISH PODS.

Salt and dry them in the sun; when quite dry, throw them into vinegar which has been boiled, but is quite cold.

TO PICKLE ONIONS.

Peel them, lay them in strong salt and water, which change every day for a week; then take them out, and wipe them carefully; lay at the bottom of the jar a small quantity of ginger, mace, cloves and allspice, seed pepper and a very small quantity of alum; put your onions in, and pour on cold vinegar.

TO PICKLE TOMATOES.

Tomatoes must be pickled, when ripe; put them in a jar with garlic, mustard seed, horse-radish, and spices; filling up the jar. Occasionally add a little fine salt, which being intended to preserve the tomatoes, must be in proportion to the quantity pickled. When the jar is full, pour in as much vinegar as will cover the whole. Cork it up tight, and it will keep a long time.

TO PICKLE ARTICHOKES.

Scrape the artichokes, and throw them into water until all are scraped; take them out, and pack them in a jar or other vessel, in fine salt, and let them stand twenty-four or thirty-six hours; then take them out, expose them to the sun for one or two days, wash them in vinegar, and put them into fresh vinegar to remain.

Mangoes or melons are to be cut in half and pickled in the same manner.

TO PICKLE WALNUTS.

Take one hundred walnuts, and run a needle through them, put them into as much beer vinegar and salt, as will cover them; let them remain in that three weeks, then take them out, drain and wipe them well; take as much white wine vinegar as will cover the walnuts, and make the pickle with a quarter of an ounce of mace, ditto of cloves, three pieces of root ginger, a nutmeg, broken into pieces, and a few peppers; boil all together, and pour it hot upon the walnuts; put two cloves of garlic with your nuts, but do not boil them; keep them dry and closely covered; mustard seed, if liked, may be added.

UNIVERSAL PICKLE.

To six quarts of vinegar, one pound of salt, a quarter of a pound of ginger, one ounce of mace, half a pound of shalots; one table-spoonful of cayenne pepper, two ounces of white pepper, two ounces of mustard seed; boil these with the vinegar, and when cold, put it into a jar; you may put in whatever green fruit or vegetables you please, fresh gathered from time to time, only wiping off the dust. If you put in carrots, they should be half boiled.

TO PICKLE MUSHROOMS.

Peel the mushroom buttons, and gently scrape the tops, which are rather yellow; wash them in cold water, put them into a stew-pan, sprinkle over them a little salt, cover close, and put them over a very slow fire; in a few minutes there will exude a liquor, then take it from the fire and shake it well; take the mushrooms from this liquor, and throw it away; let them cool, then squeeze them quite dry, through a thin cloth, and put them in bottles, and pour over them vinegar; as they imbibe the vinegar, fill up the bottles. The pickle is made in the following manner: boil three quarts of vinegar, with a handful of pimento, half an ounce of root ginger, cut small, and a little mace, cover close, and let it boil fifteen minutes; pour it over the mushrooms when quite cold; put the ginger and mace in the bottles also.

WALNUT CATSUP.

One hundred green walnuts, picked when about the size of an olive; pound them, and press out the liquor; boil it with an ounce of clove, an ounce of black pepper, and one of allspice, half an ounce of nutmegs, and half an ounce of mace, until it becomes of a fine claret color; then add one gallon of vinegar, two dozen shalots, and a table-spoonful of salt; strain through a coarse cloth, and put into bottles, well sealed, as it improves with age.

MUSHROOM CATSUP.

Gather your mushrooms early in the morning, wipe them very clean, break them in pieces, and lay them in a dry stone, or earthen vessel, with a good deal of fine salt, for twelve or fifteen hours; then squeeze them very dry in a cloth, and give the liquor one or two good boils, with a few cloves, a little mace, and allspice, let it cool and bottle it.

Take the mushrooms that have been squeezed, and dry them with a little spice, then powder them for any made dishes.

TOMATO CATSUP. No. 1.

Let your tomatoes be perfectly ripe; put them in a shallow *tin* pan; add salt, a few slices of onions, and some pods of red pepper, seasoning to your taste; stew on a slow fire until the juice is almost a jelly; then rub the mixture through a hair sieve; let it remain until the next day; then bottle it, adding a wineglass of the best port wine to each quart of the mixture. The bottles must be sealed carefully. The tomatoes should be stewed without being peeled.

16*

TOMATO CATSUP. No. 2.

Select the ripest tomatoes; scald and peel them; to one gallon tomatoes, add one quart of sharp vinegar; also, the following ingredients ground fine, viz: two table-spoonfuls of salt, one of black pepper, one of allspice, three of mustard, eight or ten pods of red pepper, one or two cloves of garlic (sliced). The whole is then put into a tin or copper kettle; simmer it over the fire three or four hours, stirring occasionally. It should then be rubbed through a sieve, fine enough to catch the seeds. Bottle it. If the simmering has not been sufficient, it will be known in a few days by the appearance of a white scum in the neck of the bottles, which can be corrected by simmering it an hour or two more, adding as much vinegar as will supply the previous loss by evaporation. The bottles should be sealed.

SOY.

Take a common sized pot of anchovies, bruise and strain them; add a quart of mushroom catsup, a quart of walnut pickle, a gallon of Madeira wine, and a little black mustard seed; boil half an hour, bottle, and cork tight; seal with wax, and in ten days the soy will be fit for use.

TEA CAKES, ETC.

A BROWN CAKE.

ONE pound of flour, one pound of butter, half a pound of powdered sugar, six eggs, half a pint of yeast, one-fourth of a pint of cream, three dessert-spoonfuls of brandy, half a nutmeg and two ounces of caraway seed, which must be steeped one night in white wine. Melt the butter, and beat the yeast into it; then the sugar, cream and eggs (which must be first beaten); then stir in the brandy, nutmeg, seed and flour. Bake in rather a quick oven.

WATER CAKE.

Three-fourths of a pound of sugar and one gill of water put together and made scalding hot; seven eggs (two whites left out); beat the eggs light while the sugar is scalding; then mix together and beat until it is very light, and rises and thickens in the beating; then sift in half a pound of flour, and stir without beating; put it into a pan, cover it with paper (not buttered), and bake one hour in a quick oven.

ORANGE CAKE.

One pound of sugar, three-fourths of a pound of butter, one pound of flour, eight eggs, the grated peel of four sweet oranges, a wineglass of orange-flower water; rub the butter and sugar to a cream, beat the eggs very light (whites and yolks separately), and add them, alternately with the flour, to the butter and sugar; then rub in the peel and essence; turn out the mixture upon a pasteboard, roll it thin and cut into shapes. Bake on tin sheets, in a moderate oven.

GATEAU À LA MADELEINE.

One pound of sifted flour, one pound of powdered sugar, half a pound of butter, eight eggs, the grated peel of four lemons and the juice of two; rub the butter and sugar to a cream; add alternately the flour and egg, which must first be beaten very light; then stir in the peel and juice. Bake in a moderate oven. The cakes should not be more than an inch thick.

KISS CAKES.

One pound of powdered loaf sugar, the whites of twelve eggs, three dessert-spoonfuls of rose-water; beat the whites to a stiff froth, and add the sugar and rose-water, beating hard all the time. Drop the mixture from a spoon upon white paper, and bake in a quick oven.

LOVE CAKES.

The yolks of twelve eggs, a glass of rose-water, one-fourth of a pound of bitter almonds, finely pounded;

enough sugar to make the batter sufficiently thick to
be baked in paper boxes. A moderate oven.

POLAND CAKES.

Four eggs, one pound of sugar, one pound of flour;
put the sugar and eggs, with a teaspoonful of mace,
over the fire; when warm, put them with the flour,
and mix well together; roll them out, and cut as
fancy directs. Bake in an oven almost cold.

LADY CAKE.

Half a pound of butter, half a pound of sugar, half
a pound of flour, half a pound of blanched almonds,
one gill of rose-water, whites of eight eggs; pound the
almonds very fine, and mix them with the flour. Make
it like pound-cake.

ARROW-ROOT SPONGE CAKE.

Sift well together half a pound of arrow-root and
one pound of sugar; beat up the whites and yolks of
seven eggs separately, and mix them together; then
stir them well, but gradually, into the arrow-root and
sugar. Flavor with lemon or rose-water to your taste.

RICE SPONGE CAKE.

Ten ounces of powdered sugar, half a pound of rice
flour, the yolks of fifteen eggs and the whites of seven,
the grated rind of two lemons, a little orange-flower

or peach water; beat the yolks for half an hour, and then add the sugar and flour, and the essences; beat the whites of the seven eggs very light, and stir them in. Pour the mixture into a deep pan, and bake immediately in a quick oven.

ALMOND SPONGE CAKE.

Pound finely in a mortar one pound of blanched almonds with the whites of three eggs; then add one pound of sifted loaf sugar, some grated lemon-peel, and the yolks of fifteen eggs; mix well together. Whip up to a solid froth the whites of twelve eggs; stir them well into the other ingredients, with a quarter of a pound of sifted wheat flour, dried. Prepare a mould, and fill it about three-fourths with the mixture. Bake it an hour in a slow oven.

SPONGE CAKE.

Ten eggs, the weight of these in sugar, and rather less than half the weight in flour; mix together the sugar and the yolks of the eggs; beat the whites *very* light, and add them; stir in the flour very lightly, when ready to bake; flavor with half a wineglass of rose-water, half of brandy, and half a nutmeg (grated), or a spoonful of vanilla, or any other essence.

MY SPONGE CAKE.

Ten eggs, a pound of sugar, half a pound of

flour, a glass of rose or peach-water, or the grated
peel and juice of a lemon; beat the eggs and sugar
very well together; add the whites, beaten as hard as
possible; sift in the flour; flavor, and bake immediately.   The pan must be well buttered.   If made in
winter, all the ingredients should be warmed, and not
allowed to grow cold before being put in the oven.

A FRENCH CAKE.

Take twelve eggs, leave out half the whites, and
beat the rest very light; put to them three-fourths of
a pound of powdered sugar, the grated peel of a lemon,
four ounces of sweet and one ounce of bitter almonds
(blanched and pounded), one pound of wheat flour,
dried and sifted.   Beat all together for an hour, and
bake an hour and ten minutes.

A RICE CAKE.

Six ounces of wheat flour, six ounces of rice flour,
three-fourths of a pound of powdered sugar, nine eggs,
one table-spoonful of orange and one of rose-water,
the grated peel of a lemon.   Beat these ingredients together for an hour, and bake an hour.

CUP CAKE.

Five tea-cupsful of flour, three of sugar, two of
milk, one of melted butter, a tea-spoonful of soda

melted in the milk, flavor as is most agreeable to your-self : mix and drop upon tin sheets.

COMPOSITION CAKE.

Seven eggs, five cups of wheat flour, three of sugar, two of butter, one tea-spoon (not heaped) of pearlash, dissolved in a cup of milk, and one nutmeg ; rub the butter and sugar to a cream; beat the eggs light, and add them gradually to the butter and sugar ; then add the flour and nutmeg ; and lastly the milk and pearlash with a glass of brandy or wine. Fruit may be added, if desired.

MEASURE CAKE.

Four tea-cups of wheat flour, three of sugar, half a cup of butter, four eggs, two table-spoonfuls of brandy, two of blanched and powdered peach-kernels ; rub the butter and sugar to a cream ; beat the eggs, and add them by degrees ; then the flour, kernels and brandy.

SCOTCH CAKE.

One cup of sugar, one of butter, two of wheat flour, and a little spice ; rub the butter and sugar together ; add the flour and spice ; roll thin ; cut with a tumbler ; and bake on tin sheets.

PORTUGAL CAKES.

Take a pound of dry flour and a pound of white

sugar powdered, mix them together, and rub a pound of butter until it is very soft and smooth, and by degrees throw in the flour and sugar, working it the whole time ; when half is in, add the yolks of six, and the whites of two eggs ; then work in the rest of the flour and sugar just before putting into the oven ; add four spoonfuls of rose-water, a little powdered mace, or if you like a pound of dried currants ; slightly butter the pans, fill them half full, press them that they may spread, dust some fine sugar over them. A quarter of an hour bakes them.

SHREWSBERRY CAKES. No. 1.

One pound of sugar, powdered ; twelve ounces of butter, one gill of cream, four eggs, a little spice, and a table-spoonful of rose (or peach) water ; rub the butter and sugar to a cream ; add the eggs, which must be first beaten quite light ; then the cream, spice, and essence, and knead in just flour enough to roll them thin ; cut out the paste in whatever shapes you please, and bake them on tins, in a slow oven.

SHREWSBERRY CAKES. No. 2.

Four eggs, a pound of flour, three quarters of a pound of sugar, half a pound of butter, a dessert-spoonful of powdered mace or cinnamon, as liked best ; mix well together, make it into little cakes, and bake on tin sheets.

17

ALDERNEY CAKES.

A cup full of brown sugar, ditto of butter, a glass of fresh milk, with a tea-spoonful of soda stirred in ; nutmeg—enough flour to make it stiff; roll out *very* thin ; cut with a tumbler, and bake in a quick oven.

———

SHORT JOURNEY CAKE

One pound of white sugar, one table-spoonful of butter, two of lard, three eggs ; rub these ingredients well together in a mortar, with as much flour as will make it of a consistency to spread upon a tin sheet about a quarter of an inch thick ; bake it until quite crisp. Peach or rose-water, or any other essence, may be used as a flavor. A little spice is sometimes added.

———

SHORT CAKE.

One pound of wheat flour, one pound of loaf sugar, three-quarters of a pound of butter, ten eggs, and a little salt ; rub the butter and sugar together ; beat the eggs light, and add them alternately with the flour to the butter and sugar; then add the salt ; bake in a loaf, in a moderate oven.

———

SODA CAKES.

Half a pound of sugar, half a pound of butter, one pint of fresh milk, one tea-spoonful of soda, and two pounds of wheat flour ; dissolve the sugar and soda in the milk, and stir in the flour ; melt the butter, and add it; then knead till quite light; put into shallow moulds, and bake quickly.

LITTLE CAKES.

To a quarter of a pound of flour, add the same quantity of butter and of sugar, and as much yolk of egg as will mix it into a stiff paste; roll them thin, and cut them with a small cup; put in caraway seeds, and bake them.

INDIAN POUND CAKE.

Half a pound of butter, the weight of eight eggs in sugar, and the weight of six in corn meal, sifted; eight eggs and a nutmeg, or a tea-spoonful of cinnamon; rub the butter and sugar to a cream; beat the eggs very light, and stir them, alternately with the meal, into the butter and sugar; add the spice, and bake in a moderate oven.

CORN CAKE.

One pint of mixed corn and wheat flour, a tea-cup of brown sugar, a table-spoonful of butter, four eggs, one nutmeg, with a little brandy.

LOAF CAKE.

Three gills of loaf sugar, three eggs, one table-spoon ful of butter. The butter, sugar and yolks of the eggs to be beaten together; beat the whites to a light froth, one gill of milk with half a tea-spoonful of soda dissolved in it, five gills of flour—season with rose or peach-water, and last of all add a dessert-spoonful of vinegar; bake in a quick oven.

PLUM CAKE FOR WEDDINGS.

Twenty pounds of butter, twenty pounds of sugar, twenty pounds of flour, twenty pounds of raisins, forty pounds of currants, twelve pounds of citron, twenty nutmegs, five ounces of mace, four ounces of cinnamon, twenty glasses of wine, twenty glasses of brandy, ten eggs to the pound; add cloves to your taste. If you wish it richer, add two pounds of currants, and one pound of raisins to each pound of flour.

FAMILY PLUM CAKE.

One and a half pounds of wheat flour, one and a quarter pounds of sugar, two pounds of currants, one pound of citron, one pound of raisins (chopped fine), three-fourths of a pound of butter, six eggs, one pint of milk or clabber, one wineglass of brandy, one nutmeg, a little mace, a few cloves, and a tea-spoonful of salæratus; rub the butter and sugar to a cream; add two eggs (well beaten), and the other ingredients, except the salæratus; beat hard for fifteen minutes; then add the salæratus, and bake at once.

POUND CAKE.

One pound of butter, one pound of sugar, one pound of flour, ten eggs, a glass of brandy, a glass of rose-water, a nutmeg (grated); rub the butter and sugar to a cream; beat the whites and yolks separately, very light, and add to the sugar and butter; stir in the flour, brandy, rose-water and nutmeg; put immediately in a quick oven, and bake two hours.

GINGER POUND CAKE.

Ten eggs, one pound of butter, one pound of brown sugar, one pound of flour, one pint of molasses, two cups of strong ginger, the rind of two lemons and the juice of one, a wineglass of brandy, a wineglass of rose-water, one nutmeg and a tea-spoonful of ground mace. If you want it very nice, add two pounds of currants. Beat the butter and sugar together; add the eggs, after having beaten them very light, separately; add the molasses and other ingredients for flavoring; last of all, the flour. Bake.

GINGER CAKE. No. 1.

One pound of butter, three-fourths of a pound of sugar (brown), one and a half pints of molasses, two eggs, one and a half ounces of ginger, one table-spoonful of the spices—cinnamon, mace, cloves and allspice; wheat flour to make it stiff enough to roll into thin sheets. Rub the butter and sugar to a cream; add the eggs, and then the other ingredients at will,

17*

rèserving a portion of the flour to knead in, after the
mixture has been turned out upon the pasteboard.
Cut into shapes, and bake on tin sheets, in a quick
oven.

GINGER CAKE. No. 2.

Half a pound of brown sugar, two ounces of butter,
one ounce of ginger, three and a half gills of molasses,
one table-spoonful of orange marmalade, one pound of
wheat flour, and caraway seeds to the taste. Mix the
ingredients well together, and bake in plates.

HAMPTON GINGER CAKE.

A teacup of molasses, one of sugar (brown), one of
butter, three of flour, three eggs, a table-spoonful of
powdered ginger, and a tea-spoonful of salæratus;
rub the butter and sugar to a cream; beat the eggs
light, and add them; then stir in the molasses, ginger,
flour, and lastly the salæratus, which must be first dissolved in a little water or milk. Bake in a pan.

LAFAYETTE GINGER CAKE.

One and a half pounds of wheat flour, quarter of a
pound of butter, one pint of molasses, one pint of
brown sugar, ten eggs, ginger to the taste, one tea-
spoonful of pearlash, dissolved in warm water; stir all
together, and bake in pans or patties. Currants and
raisins may be added.

THIN GINGER BREAD.

Put in a bowl a pint of treacle or best boiled molasses, a pint of brown sugar, three good spoonfuls of butter, a table-spoonful of ginger, the same of powdered allspice, and two spoonfuls of grated orange-peel ; stir all together well, and mix in about a pint of wheat flour ; turn all out on the bread-board, and roll it thin with as little flour as you can to prevent its sticking, (this will require about a quart of flour); cut in long, narrow slips, and bake on tin sheets.

SUGAR GINGER BREAD.

Two pounds of flour, one and a half pounds of sugar (brown), one pound of butter, nine eggs, one cup of powdered ginger, and a cup of wine ; rub the butter and sugar to a cream ; beat the eggs and add them ; stir in the flour, ginger and wine.

SEED GINGER BREAD.

One pound of flour, half a pound of sugar, two ounces of butter, one ounce of ginger, half a pint of molasses ; marmalade, seeds and citron to your taste.

POLKA GINGER BREAD.

To a pint of good molasses add a pound of butter, a pound of brown sugar, two table-spoonfuls of pounded ginger, half a tea-spoonful of pearlash, and as much flour as will knead it into a stiff paste ; roll it out very thin, and cut into cakes; bake on tin sheets, in a quick oven. Citron pared thin may be added, and any spice you may fancy.

MARION CAKE.

One and a half pounds of wheat flour, half a pound of butter, half a pound of brown sugar, one pint of molasses or treacle, five eggs, one tea-spoonful of supercarbonate of soda, two large table-spoonfuls of powdered ginger, two of powdered orange-peel, one dozen and a half of cloves, one dozen and a half of allspice, one tea-spoonful of mace, and some cinnamon. Stir all these ingredients well together; the soda, dissolved in a little water, should be added last. Bake in patties.

SWEET CROQUETTES.

Take one pound of powdered sugar, one pound of butter, half a pound of wheat flour, half a pound of corn flour; mix all together; add the juice and grated peel of a large lemon, or any other flavoring that you prefer; make it into a lump of dough; then put it into a mortar and beat it hard on both sides; roll it out thin, and cut it in cakes with the edge of a tumbler; flour a tin sheet and lay the cakes on, but not close together; bake them about ten minutes, and grate sugar over them when done.

APEES.

Half a pound of flour, quarter of a pound of butter,

half a glass of wine, with a table-spoonful of rose-water mixed with it, one-fourth of a pound of white sugar, half a nutmeg, a tea-spoonful of cinnamon and mace, and one and a half table-spoonfuls of caraway seed ; mix the butter in the flour ; add the caraway, sugar and spice ; pour in the liquor by degrees ; add enough cold water to make a stiff dough ; spread some flour on the paste-board, take the dough and knead it well ; cut it into the flour, and knead each piece ; put all together and knead again ; roll out into a thin sheet, and cut into cakes ; bake in a Dutch oven a few minutes. The top of the oven should be hotter than the bottom.

MARGUERITES.

Beat together until very light, one pound of butter, and one pound of sugar ; sift a pound of flour, take the yolks of twelve eggs, and beat them until very thick and smooth ; pour them into the flour, and add the beaten butter and sugar ; stir in a grated nutmeg, and a wine-glass of rose-water ; mix the whole together until it becomes a lump of dough ; flour the paste board, and lay the dough upon it, sprinkle it with flour and roll it out about half an inch thick, and cut it into round cakes ; flour a tin, put the cakes on so as not to touch and bake them five minutes in a quick oven ; if too cold the cakes will run ; when the cakes are cold lay on each a large lump of currant or other fruit jelly ; take the whites of the eggs, and beat them until they stand alone ; then add sugar enough to make the consistency of icing; flavor it with anything you like, heap up with a spoon a pile of icing on each cake over the jelly; set them in a cool oven till the icing becomes firm and of a pale brown color.

JUMBLES.

One pound of wheat flour, one pound of loaf sugar, three-quarters of a pound of butter, the whites of six eggs; rub the butter and sugar to a cream; beat in the egg, which must be first frothed, and then the flour; then add a wineglass of rose or peach-water, a powdered nutmeg, a tea-spoonful of powdered mace and cinnamon. Turn it out upon your board; cut it into small pieces, and roll each one separately in a little flour and sugar; lay them upon sheets, and bake in a slow oven.

Shrewsberry cakes are made in the same way, except that, instead of being rolled, the mixture is dropped upon the sheets.

JUMBLES. No. 2.

Three eggs, one pound of flour, ditto of loaf sugar, half pound of butter, a wineglass of rose-water, ten drops of essence of lemon, one tea-spoonful of cinnamon; beat the butter and sugar together; add the eggs beaten light, rose-water, &c., &c., &c.; bake in a slow oven.

JUMBLES. No. 3.

One pound of butter, two pounds of white sugar,

one stick of cinnamon, one nutmeg, one glass of rose (or peach) water, the yolks of eight eggs ; rub the butter and sugar to a cream ; beat the eggs very light, and add them to the butter and sugar ; then the spice and essence ; then stir in enough well dried wheat flour to make the mixture stiff enough to roll ; twist your jumbles, dip them in powdered sugar, and bake on a tin sheet.

MACAROONS. No. 1.

One pound of sweet almonds, and half a pound of bitter, blanched and pounded until fine in a marble mortar, with half a glass of rose-water ; then add one and a half pounds of powdered loaf sugar, and the whites of four eggs whipped to a stiff froth ; beat all well together, and drop a dessert-spoonful of the mixture at a time upon a grated paper or upon tin sheets ; bake in a slow oven.

MACAROONS. No. 2.

To half a pound of sweet almonds, and a fourth of bitter (pounded) ; add three-quarters of a pound of loaf sugar ; beat the whites of three eggs, and mix them with a little rose-water into the almonds and sugar. When the mixture is of the right consistency, drop by spoonfuls on tin sheets, and bake in a slow oven.

MARVELLE. No. 1.

Five table-spoonfuls of melted butter or lard, six of

sugar, four eggs, and a tea-spoonful of salæratus—wheat flour to make it stiff enough to knead. After kneading well, roll thin; cut into pieces, and fry in boiling lard. Spices, and rose, or peach-water may be added, if desired.

MARVELLE. No. 2.

One pound of sugar, ten eggs, a little orange-peel and cinnamon powdered; beat the eggs very light, and add the sugar to them with the spices, and as much flour as will make the dough stiff enough to roll out to the thickness of a quarter of an inch. Shape the cakes with a jagging iron, and fry in boiling lard.

SWEET WAFERS. No. 1.

Half a pound of white sugar (or brown), half a pound of wheat flour, a quarter of a pound of butter, eight eggs, four table-spoonfuls of peach or rose-water; beat the eggs very light, whites and yolks separately; rub the butter and sugar to a cream; add the eggs to it; then beat in the flour, essence, and a little powdered cinnamon and nutmeg. As soon as taken out of the oven, they must be rolled up.

SWEET WAFERS. No. 2.

Three eggs, a small tea-cup of cream, the same of sugar, a little wheat flour, a little citron, minced very fine, a little rose-water, brandy and cinnamon; beat these ingredients together, very light; rub over your wafer-iron with lard, put in a spoonful of the mixture, bake both sides, and roll the wafers as soon as taken out of the iron.

ALMOND BISCUITS.

Half a pound of almonds, blanched and pounded very fine, with as much rose (or orange-flower) water as will prevent their oiling; the yolks of eight, and the whites of four eggs, beaten until very light, and added to the almonds; then beat in three-quarters of a pound of loaf sugar; continue to beat while the oven is heating. When ready, add three ounces of wheat flour, which must be just stirred in, and not beaten; butter your pans, and fill them about half full; dust a little sugar over them when in the oven, which must be a moderate one.

RATAFIA BISCUITS.

Take half a pound of peach-kernels, or bitter almonds; blanch and beat them very fine with an equal quantity of loaf sugar; make it into a pretty stiff paste with the white of an egg (frothed); roll the Biscuit about the size of a nutmeg; lay them on paper, and bake in a slow oven.

SPONGE BISCUITS.

Beat the yolks of twelve eggs half an hour; then add one and a half pounds of finely powdered sugar,

18

and beat until bubbles rise ; beat the whites very light, and add them ; then stir in fourteen ounces of wheat (or rice) flour, and the grated rinds of two lemons. Bake in tin moulds in a quick oven.

DROP BISCUITS.

Beat eight eggs very light ; add to them one pound of sugar, and twelve ounces of wheat flour ; when perfectly light, add some well powdered coriander seed. Then drop on tin sheets, and bake.

INN BISCUITS.

One pound of flour, half a pound of sugar, half a pound of butter, one glass of wine or brandy, a little spice ; rub the butter and sugar together ; add the other ingredients, and when well kneaded, wet the dough with milk ; roll it out and cut into shape. Bake quickly.

SWEET ROLLS.

Take a pound of flour, dry it, add a table-spoonful of fine moist sugar, and a lump of butter as big as an egg ; wet it with milk and two spoonfuls of yeast. Bake this in a quick oven. If large rolls, a quarter of an hour will be sufficient. You must not knead or roll them, but cut them and lay them on tins. The dough will rise in ten minutes.

SALLY LUNN.

Two eggs, two small cups of cream, two cups of loaf sugar, one pint of flour, half a pound of butter, one tea-spoonful of mace ; the cream and butter to be warmed together, and when well melted, to be poured into the eggs and sugar, which must be well beaten together ; sift the flour into it gradually, add a tea-spoonful of tartaric acid, one and a half tea-spoonfuls of soda ; the soda must be dissolved in warm water, and mixed in well.   Have the pans buttered and the oven ready ; then stir the acid in quickly ; put into the oven immediately, before the effervescence ceases.

TEA BREAD. No. 1.

Two table-spoonfuls of white sugar, two of butter, one of wheat flour, one teacup of leaven, two eggs, a little salt and a little water ; rub the butter and sugar together ; beat the eggs light and add them, with the other ingredients.   Make into a loaf, and bake in a pan.

TEA BREAD. No. 2.

One and a half pounds of bread dough, three-fourths of a pound of loaf sugar, six ounces of butter, five eggs, one dessert-spoonful of powdered cinnamon, half a teaspoonful of soda, dissolved in a tea-cup of milk ; put these ingredients into a bowl, and beat them to a batter ; then put the batter into baking-pans, sprinkle loaf sugar and a few small lumps of butter over the top, and bake in a moderate oven.

RUSKS. No. 1.

Five eggs, five ounces of butter, three-fourths of a pound of sugar, half a pint of milk, half a pint of strong yeast; rub the butter and sugar to a cream; add the eggs, and continue to beat; when quite light, add the yeast and milk; then stir in enough flour to make a thick batter. Set the mixture in some covered vessel (the same in which it is mixed is to be preferred) in a warm place to rise. When very light, knead in flour enough to roll it into balls; put them upon tin sheets, and set them to rise again. When quite light, bake in a moderate oven.

These rusks are very nice, split and dried, in a very slow oven till crisped throughout.

RUSKS. No. 2.

Two pounds of flour, six ounces of sugar, half a pound of currants, one gill of yeast, and boiled milk (cold) enough to make it into a dough that you can knead; let it rise; make it up into forms, and bake. If you wish it very light, do not mix the dough stiff enough to knead at first, but keep back part of the flour, and knead it in when the soft dough has risen three or four hours; then set it to rise a second time, and when sufficiently risen, bake.

RUSKS. No. 3.

Half a pound of flour, one gill of yeast, a gill and a half of boiled milk (cold); mixed at night. In the morning the yolks of three eggs and the whites of two, well beaten with half a pound of loaf sugar and a moderate spoonful of butter; then stir in what you mixed over night, and add half a pound of flour; knead the rusk or not, as you please, but add no more flour; the white of the egg will do to glaze the top.

BUNNS. No. 1.

Rub into two and a quarter pounds of sifted wheat flour half a pound of fresh butter; beat two eggs with half a pound of white sugar; mix them with one pint of new milk (warmed) and one gill of very light yeast; stir all together into the flour, and set it to rise; when very light, turn the dough out upon a paste-board, cut with a cup or wineglass, put the Bunns upon tin sheets, and let them rise again. Bake them twenty minutes in a quick oven.

BUNNS. No. 2.

Beat light three eggs; add half a pint of milk, one spoonful of butter, and flour for a moderately thin batter. Bake it in tin cups, in a quick oven.

WIGS. No. 1.

Two pounds of wheat flour, half a pound of butter, half a pound of sugar, one pint of milk; mix these ingredients well together, and add three table-spoonfuls of good yeast, a little cinnamon and rose-water;

18*

cover the mixture, and set it in a warm place to rise; when light, bake in rings, and split and butter them while hot.

WIGS. No. 2.

Five eggs to a quart of milk, warmed; a large spoonful of butter melted in the milk; one of sugar; in winter, three spoonfuls of yeast; in summer, two; thicken it with flour to a stiff batter, and bake on a griddle with rings.

BUTTERMILK BREAD.

One quart of wheat flour, one dessert-spoonful (not heaped) of supercarbonate of soda, one table-spoonful of butter, half a pound of powdered sugar, a tumbler and a half of buttermilk; mix these ingredients, and knead them into a soft dough, which place in a greased pan, and set it to rise in a slightly warmed Dutch oven; when risen, bake. This bread keeps a long time, and makes excellent toast.

POTATO CORN BREAD.

One quart of fine corn meal, half a pint of milk, half a pound of sweet potatoes, half a pound of butter, one pound of brown sugar, and eight eggs; boil and mash smooth the potatoes, rub the butter and sugar to a cream, and add them to the potatoes; beat the eggs and stir them into the butter, &c. &c.; then add the milk, and lastly the meal; beat the whole well together, and bake in a pan.

SWEET CORN BREAD.

A pint of corn meal unwashed, half a pint of milk, half a pint of molasses, a table-spoonful of butter, and one of powdered ginger—two eggs; beat the eggs light, and add the other ingredients—the meal last. Bake in a pan.

QUEEN ESTHER'S BREAD.

Cut some slices of bread, and lay them in milk for some hours. Then beat two eggs; dip the slices in the egg, and fry them. When of a nice brown, pour over them any syrup you please, and serve up.

DIET BREAD.

Nine eggs, one pound of sugar, fourteen ounces of flour,—beat the yolks with a whisk till quite thick; then mix the sugar with them and beat till light; beat the whites well, and add them by degrees; put the flour in gradually; bake in a quick oven.

SWEET POTATO WAFFLES.

Two table-spoonfuls of mashed potato, one of butter, one of sugar, one pint of milk, four table-spoonfuls of wheat flour; mix these ingredients well together, and bake in a waffle iron.

RAISED WAFFLES.

Make a thick batter of milk and flour, add four eggs

beat light, a gill of yeast, a spoonful of butter; let it rise some hours. As you take them out of the iron— butter, and sprinkle them with cinnamon and sugar.

WAFFLES.

Thicken half a pint of milk with four spoonfuls of flour; when cold, add another half pint of milk, a spoonful of butter, the yolks of three eggs; mix these well together; the whites of the eggs must be beaten to a froth, and stirred in immediately before baking; butter them as you take them from the iron.

RICE FLANNEL-CAKES.

Half a pint of soft boiled rice, a tea-cup of cream, a tea-cup of sugar, three eggs, a table-spoonful of yeast, or a tea-spoonful of pearlash. Let the rice cool, and add the other ingredients, rubbing them well together; bake on a griddle.

COCOA-NUT PUFFS.

Two cocoa-nuts, peeled and grated, three-quarters of a pound of powdered sugar, the whites of two eggs, frothed, one table-spoonful of powdered cinnamon, one nutmeg, grated, one table-spoonful of rose-water, two tea-spoonfuls of butter; mix the ingredients well together, and make into small cones—say about double the size of a thimble. Put these on tin sheets, and *dry* them thoroughly in the oven. Next day ice them, and they will be fit for use.

COCOA-NUT DROPS.

Twelve eggs to five cocoa-nuts ; grate the nuts fine, and dry it in a moderate oven ; beat up the whites of the eggs ; then add the sugar (allowing one cup to two of the cocoa-nut), and beat to a paste ; then stir in the cocoa-nut, and drop on a pan or on a sheet of paper, and bake for ten or fifteen minutes.

RAISED LOAF CAKE.

Six pounds of flour, three pounds of butter, three pounds of sugar, one pint of wine, one pint of brandy, one pint of milk, one quart of yeast, twelve eggs, three ounces of spice, and five pounds of fruit ; rub the butter and sugar to a cream ; beat the eggs very light (whites and yolks separately), and add them alternately, with the flour ; then the other ingredients, beating hard all the time ; pour it into a pan, and set it to rise ; when very light—bake.

RAISED DOUGH-NUTS.

One pint of milk, one pint of yeast, one pound of sugar, half a pound of butter, four eggs, and flour to thicken it ; rub the butter and sugar to a cream ; beat the eggs very light, and add then the milk, yeast, and flour ; make into nuts, and bake on tin sheets.

MISCELLANEOUS.

THE FRENCH MODE OF MAKING POULTRY TENDER.

Kill whatever you wish to dress the evening before, and throw it immediately into cold water. In that let it remain all night, and the next morning pick and prepare your turkey, fowl, or any other poultry, in the usual manner.

TO PICKLE BEEF OR PORK.

Take one hundred pounds of beef, or pork—wash it well in cold water, and let it drip ; take five quarts of salt, and four pounds of brown sugar, four ounces of saltpetre ; rub these ingredients together, and then well into the meat ; pack it close in a barrel, and place a heavy weight on it. In three weeks it will be fit for use.

AN EXCELLENT RECEIPT FOR PICKLING TONGUES, BEEF, PORK, ETC.

To one ounce of saltpetre, add four quarts of salt, and half a pound of brown sugar ; mix all well together, and rub on the meat, every other day for a week ; turning, and letting it remain in its own pickle, kept close from the air. The tongues must be soaked in cold water for twelve hours, to draw out the blood. This mixture will be enough for twelve pieces.

TO PICKLE SHRIMPS.

Pick your shrimps, and rinse them well in salt and water; take *two* parts of strong vinegar, and *one* of water, add a few allspice, and boil this pickle; pour it hot over the shrimps. If the shrimps are to be sent to a distance, the pickle should be boiled again; adding a little more vinegar, and pouring it on the shrimps hot, again. They must be entirely covered by the pickle; a paper wet with brandy, should be placed over the top. They will thus keep sound a long time.

FOR PICKLING SHRIMPS. No. 2.

Ten plates of shrimps to be boiled and peeled; for which quantity prepare an ounce of mace, an ounce of cinnamon, half an ounce of white pepper; of alum and saltpetre each about the size of a nutmeg. The above to be boiled in a gallon of vinegar, and when perfectly cold, to be poured over the shrimps.

TO POT SHRIMPS.

Pick the shrimps (after they are boiled) from the shells; beat them well in a mortar, and put as much melted butter to them as will make them of the proper consistence to be pressed compactly together; add pepper, salt, mace and nutmeg to the taste; put the mixture into small pans, and pour melted butter over them about quarter of an inch thick. If wanted for immediate use, grated bread may be added.

TO PICKLE OYSTERS.

Be careful to save the liquor when opening your oysters, and scald them in it; take them out of the liquor, and to one and a half pints of it add two pints of vinegar, one pint of Madeira wine, and some mace; boil these ingredients together for half an hour, skimming carefully, and pour hot over the oysters.

TO CURE DRUM ROES.

Have the roes carefully washed in cold water; put them into a tray, and sprinkle some pounded salt over them. The next day pour off the pickle which has been formed, and again sprinkle salt over them. Repeat this the third day, after which the roes must be put on a board, in the sun, to dry; no pressing is needed. To each roe allow two ounces of salt at every salting. When perfectly dry, wrap them in paper, and hang them up in a dry room.

Mullet roes are cured in the same way.

TO CURE HAMS AND BACON.

To five hogs allow one pound of saltpetre (powdered), three quarts of molasses, and enough pounded common salt to rub the meat thoroughly. Let the pieces lie together, if the weather is warm, three days; if cold, they may remain a day or two longer. Then rub them again with salt only. At the end of eight days pour from them the brine, and rub them again

19

with the salt that remains about them ; and if there is not enough of this, use a little more, with powdered red pepper. Unless the weather makes one apprehensive, there will be no occasion to touch them again. Let them lie in the brine for three weeks ; then smoke till they are well dried.

FOR SAUSAGES.

To fifteen pounds of meat (nine pounds lean to six pounds fat), picked and chopped fine, add half a pint of salt, a table-spoonful of saltpetre (finely powdered), two spoonfuls of dried sage, two spoonfuls of powdered thyme, half a pound of pepper, half a pound of allspice, one nutmeg and a pinch of mace, pounded all fine ; then season the meat and let it lie all night, and stuff it in the skins in the morning. The skins should be scraped very thin, and every little film taken off.

HOG'S HEAD CHEESE.

Take the faces of the hogs and boil them until the bones be quite loose, and can be taken out without trouble ; pick them all well out ; take the skins and lay them on a coarse cloth in a deep dish, the outside of the skin next the cloth, in the same manner as you would put paste to make an apple-dumpling. This done, season the faces well, as you would do sausages ; put it (the meat) upon the skins, of which you must have some to lay over the top; then tie it up as for a dumpling, not too tight; put it into a press or under a heavy weight for two days, when it will be fit for use.

FINES HERBS.

Take a cup full of chopped shalots or onions, a little parsley, one laurel-leaf, estragon, thyme, sweet marjorem and lemon-peel; chop them fine, and put them, with three ounces of butter, in a stew-pan over the fire; stir the mixture a short time, until the butter becomes clear; then put it in an earthen pot, where it will keep eight days sound.

AN EXCELLENT RECEIPT FOR GROUNDNUT CANDY.

To one quart of molasses add half a pint of brown sugar and a quarter of a pound of butter; boil it for half an hour over a slow fire; then put in a quart of groundnuts, parched and shelled; boil for a quarter of an hour, and then pour it into a shallow tin pan to harden.

GROUNDNUT CAKE.

One pint of parched and pounded groundnuts, one pint of brown sugar, the whites of five eggs; froth the eggs, and stir in, alternately, the sugar and nuts. Bake in patties, in a slow oven.

LEMON DROPS.

To one pound of powdered sugar add the peel and

juice of one lemon; mix these well together; then add the whites of two eggs, well beaten, to the sugar and lemon; rub the whole in a marble mortar; then roll and cut in slices, and bake on a tin sheet well sugared. The tin should be sugared as you roll.

TAFFY CANDY.

Fill a saucepan half full of coarse brown sugar; moisten it with molasses; add a table-spoonful of butter, and some lemon-juice and peel; boil your candy and pour it on well buttered tin sheets or plates. It must be very thin.

TO CANDY FLOWERS.

Take any kind of flower you think pretty; clarify and boil a pound of fine sugar until it is nearly candied; when the sugar begins to grow stiff, and rather cool, dip the flowers into it; take them out immediately, and lay them one by one on a sieve to dry.

TO CLARIFY SUGAR.

To three pounds of sugar allow the white of one egg, and a pint and a half of water; break the sugar into small lumps, put it into a saucepan and pour the water over it; let it stand some time before it is put on the fire; then add the beaten white of the egg; stir it until the sugar is entirely dissolved, and when it boils up, pour in a pint of cold water; let it boil up a second time, then take it off the fire and let it settle for fifteen minutes; carefully remove the scum; put it on the fire again, and boil it till thick enough.

————•————

COLORING FOR ICE CREAM, ETC. No. 1.

Boil very slowly in a gill of water, till reduced to half, twenty grains of cochineal; the same of alum and of cream of tartar, powdered finely; strain and keep in a phial, tightly corked. For *yellow* coloring use an infusion of saffron; for *green*, spinach leaves boiled, and the juice expressed.

————•————

COLORING FOR ICE CREAM, ETC. No. 2.

Express the juice from the pokeberry, and to every pint allow a pound of sugar, and boil fifteen minutes. A tea-spoonful of this jelly will color two quarts of milk or jelly.

THE END.

A PRELIMINARY CHECKLIST

of South Carolina Cookbooks
Published Before 1935

Southern cookbooks are a gourmet's dream and bibliographer's nightmare. Since 1900 many have been published by women's auxiliaries of one sort or another (the "publisher" being not the printer, but the one who pays the printer's bills). The variety of good causes to which the "proceeds" of such books have proceeded is moving to contemplate. Many lives have been saved by the efforts of Southern women who raised funds by collecting each other's recipes and selling them to each other, but in one's less charitable moments it is possible to be extremely vexed with the frequent failure of those ladies, and of the printers who were glad to take their money, to clearly indicate a place and year of publication in their cookbooks. In some cases one cannot even identify a title page for the book and must select a phrase from somewhere near the beginning and use it as a title.

Some of these books are exceedingly rare. The better a cookbook is the more likely its pages are to be hastily flapped, written in, and spilled upon, with the distinctly un-Darwinian result that among cookbooks it is not the fittest but the least fit that survive.

It is surprising what a story these cookbooks tell when you arrange them in chronological order. For instance, the earliest known private recipe books are family affairs, handed down from woman to woman, but the first *published* cookbooks are by men of considerable social standing. When women begin to publish their own cookbooks they are largely anonymous, no South Carolina woman being named on a title page until the twentieth century. From wealth as no other Americans had known it, South Carolinians went to poverty as no other Americans had known it, and the silence of the 1880s "speaks volumes" (has that old cliché ever been more apt?). Then the names of upcountry communities (Spartanburg, Greenville, Greenwood) begin to appear, soon followed by the Pee Dee section.

Many of the recipes were devised by blacks, of course, but it was usually whites who wrote them down, and recipes written down and published by South Carolina blacks are only a very recent development. Lastly one cannot help but see in these cookbooks the enduring importance to South Carolinians of their local churches.

It has not been practicable yet to continue the checklist beyond 1934. There was a proliferation of local cookbooks in the late '30s. I have tried to include revised editions as separate cross-referenced entries, but I have not listed routine unrevised reprints. It will be obvious that I have included a few titles that would not normally be categorized as cookbooks but which seem pertinent. There must be some inaccuracies and many omissions below, but we have to start somewhere.

1   The Domestic Encyclopedia

Or a Dictionary of Facts and Useful Knowledge. Chiefly Applicable to Rural & Domestic Economy. With an Appendix, Containing Additions in Domestic Medicine, and the Veterinary and Culinary Arts. In Three Volumes
BY A. F. M. WILLICH, M. D. Author of the Lectures on Diet & Regimen, etc.

Second American Edition, with Additions,
BY THOMAS COOPER, ESQ. M. D., Professor of Chemistry and Mineralogy
Philadelphia, Pa., 1821
> Cooper was acting President of the South Carolina College at this time.

2   A Treatise of Domestic Medicine Intended For Families

In Which the Treatments of Common Disorders are Alphabetically Enumerated. To Which is Added, a Practical System of Domestic Cookery, Describing the Best, Most Economical, and Most Wholesome Methods of Dressing Vituals; Intended for the Use of Families Who Do Not Affect Magnificence in Their Style of Living.
BY THOMAS COOPER, M. D.

Also THE ART OF PRESERVING All Kinds of Animal and Vegetable Substances for Many Years, by M. Appert.
Reading, Pa., 1824

Now established as the extremely controversial President of the college that became the University of South Carolina, Cooper evidently shared the interest of his friend Thomas Jefferson in food and drink.

3   The Carolina Receipt Book

Or Housekeeper's Assistant in Cookery, Medicine, and Other Subjects Connected with the Management of a Family.
BY A LADY OF CHARLESTON
Charleston, S.C., 1832

This is apparently a unique copy and was found with Pinckney material in *Runnymede*, Ashley River, and given to the Charleston Museum. The contents do not suggest any connection with No. 9 but it may be by Harriott Pinckney, Miss Rutledge's first cousin.

4   The Southern Gardener and Receipt Book

Containing Directions for Gardening; a Collection of Valuable Receipts for Cookery, the Preservation of Fruits and Other Articles of Household Consumption, and for the Cure of Diseases
BY P. THORNTON, of Camden, South Carolina
Columbia, S.C., 1840

The "P" stand for *Phineas*. See No. 6.

5   The Southern Farmer and Market Gardener

Being a Compilation of Useful Articles on These Subjects, from the Most Approved Writers. Developing the Principles and Pointing out the Method of their Application to the Farming and Gardening of the South, and Particularly of the Low Country.
BY FRANCIS S. HOLMES, of Charleston, S. C.
Charleston, S.C., 1842
    See also no. 12.

6   The Southern Gardener and Receipt Book

Containing Directions for Gardening; a Collection of Valuable Receipts for Cookery, the Preservation of Fruits and Other Articles of Household Consumption, and for the Cure of Diseases
BY P. THORNTON, of Camden, South Carolina
Newark, N.J., 1845
    Second edition of No. 4.

7   Carolina Sports by Land and Water

Including incidents of devil-fishing, &c
BY THE HONORABLE WILLIAM ELLIOTT
Charleston, S.C., 1846
    It is said that this classic description and defense of the hunting and fishing of the gentry around Charleston has never been out of print since it was first published. Contains a few prescriptions for the cooking of fish.

8   Medico-Botanical Catalogue

Of the Plants and Ferns of St. John's, Berkly, South Carolina. An Inaugural Thesis submitted to the Dean and Faculty of the Medical College of the State of South-Carolina for the Degree of M.D.
BY FRANCIS PEYRE PORCHER.
Charleston, S.C., 1847
    See also Nos. 13, 16, and 17. The title pages tell the story of his life and times.

9   The Carolina Housewife

Or House and Home:
BY A LADY OF CHARLESTON
Charleston, S.C., 1847

> In *The Olden Time of Carolina*, which was published in Charleston in 1855, Elizabeth Ann Poyas refers to "Miss Sally Rutledge" as the author of "that excellent volume 'The Carolina house-wife or cookery book,' which she published for charitable purposes." Its influence on later books is incalculable. *See also* Nos. 11, 14, and 20.

10   Extracts from Dr. Barratt's Notes

On the Indigenous Plants of Abbeville District, S. C.
BY HENRY R. FROST
New York, N.Y., 1850

> Pages 318–321 of the third volume of the Transactions of the American Medical Association.

11   The Carolina Housewife

Or House and Home:
BY A LADY OF CHARLESTON
The Second Edition, Revised, Enlarged, and Corrected
Charleston, S.C., 1851

> A second edition of No. 9, again published by Babcock but this time printed in Charleston on "the steam-power press of Walker & James, No. 101 East Bay." The page is less attractive, more crowded, and more Victorian than in the first edition, but most of the spellings have been normalized and some delicious recipes added, including candied almonds called "Ekboladoolas" and described as a "Hindoo Receipt." Also a professionally anonymous "Editor" turns up as the author of a "Note." More recipes in fewer pages.3

12   The Southern Farmer and Market Gardener

Being a Compilation of Useful Articles on These Subjects, from the Most Approved Writers.

BY FRANCIS S. HOLMES

New, Improved and Enlarged Edition, with a Treatise on the Cultivation of Rice and Cotton

Charleston, S.C., 1852

Brief and excellent; every angle of production noted, particularly shipping and preservation. He notes Bachman; he notes and recommends the *Isabella* or Carolina grape and the white scuppernong or Roanoke grape; he notes when to put out vegetables by the months and what to do; he notes Mr. Prince of the Linnaean Botanic Garden of Flushing, New York. There is reference to the paper read by Judge William Johnson at the Horticultural Society of Charleston but Mr. Holmes says that strawberries cannot be cultivated for the market in Charleston. He notes benne seed and says of the guinea squash that it is really blue eggplant. He notes that several varieties of mulberries are cultivated but few are fit for the table. This is a revised edition of No. 5.

13   The Medicinal, Poisonous, and Dietetic Properties, of the Cryptogamic Plants of the United States.

Being a report made to the American Medical Association, at its sessions held in Richmond, Va., and St. Louis, Mo.,

BY FRANCIS PEYRE PORCHER, M. D. One of the Editors of the Charleston Med. Jour. and Rev.; Lecturer on Mat. Med. and Therap.; Corresp. Memb. of the Lyceum of Nat. Hist. of New York, and of the Acad. of Nat. Sciences of Philadelphia.

New York, N.Y., 1854

From the Transactions of The American Medical Association, Volume VII.

14　House and Home

Or, The Carolina Housewife.
BY A LADY OF CHARLESTON
Third Edition, Corrected and Enlarged.
Charleston, S.C., 1855

> This is the third edition of No. 9 and was published the year of
> Miss Rutledge's death, possibly the reason Mrs. Poyas could use
> her name. One can but guess at the reason for the reverse of the
> title from "The Carolina Housewife or House and Home."

15　The Farmer and Planter

Devoted to Agriculture, Horticulture, Domestic and Rural Economy
Pendleton, S.C., 1856

> This was a monthly that named George Seaborn as its editor
> and proprietor, and S. W. Lewis as its publisher. Number Two
> of Volume Seven was the issue for February, 1856.

16　Resources of the Southern Fields and Forests

*Medical, Economical, and Agricultural. Being Also a Medical Botany of
the Confederate States; with Practical Information on the Useful Properties of the Trees, Plants, and Shurbs.*
BY FRANCIS PEYRE PORCHER, Surgeon P.A.C.S.
Charleston, S.C., 1863

> "P.A.C.S." stood for Provisional Army of the Confederate States.
> This 1863 publication was truly important as by that time the
> blockade restricted the importation of many drugs. *See also* No.
> 17.

17 Resources of the Southern Fields and Forests

Medical, Economical and Agricultural; being also a MEDICAL BOT-
ANY OF THE SOUTHERN STATES: *with practical information
on the useful properties of the trees, plants, and shrubs.*
BY FRANCIS PEYRE PORCHER, M. D. Formerly Surgeon in charge of
City Hospitals, Charleston; and Lecturer of Materia Medica and
Therapeutics; Corresponding Member of the Medical and Surgical
and Obstetric Societies, and the Lyceum of Natural History of New
York, and of the Academy of Natural Sciences of Philadelphia. New
Edition—Revised and Largely Augmented.
Charleston, S.C., 1869

> Uses of plants, trees, flowers, fruits, wines: careful directions of
> every sort: much on preparation of food, fresh and preserved.
> There are directions for the local favorites: heart of palm pickles,
> pumpkin chips, watermelon rind pickles, and what we call peach
> leather. Carolina rice and wild rices are gone into; as also is cot-
> ton seed oil. All varieties of apples and the making of vinegar
> and ciders. Native and imported grapes are noted at length, with
> the making of wines from grapes, from blackberries and from
> dewberries: fermentation of grains—rye, barley, corn, and oth-
> ers; the making of cordials from wild cherry and wild plums and
> a liquor from birch bark. The use of various things medicinal is
> stressed. Second edition of No. 16.

18 The Southern Gardener

*or Short and Simple Directions for the Culture of Vegetables and Fruits of
the South*
BY DR. HENRY W. RAVENEL, Aiken, S. C.
Charleston, S.C. [1871?]

19 The Centennial Receipt Book

Written in 1876
BY A SOUTHERN LADY
[Charleston, S.C.? 1877?]

20   House and Home:

Or, The Carolina House Wife,
BY A LADY OF CHARLESTON.

Fourth Edition. Corrected and Enlarged.
Charleston, S.C. Undated.
    Fourth edition of No. 9.

21   Cook Book

The Charleston Exchange for Women's Work
[Charleston, S.C.? 1895?]
    In the last quarter of the 19th century a *Cook Book* was put out
    by The Charleston Exchange for Woman's Work at 215–217
    King Street, which had been incorporated on December 1,
    1885. This small effort had a half page on the reason and neces-
    sity for such an *Exchange* and forty-odd pages of receipts, as well
    as a page of excellent culinary definitions. The whole *Exchange*
    setup, individuals as well as food, formed the pleasant back-
    ground for Owen Wister's delightful novel *Lady Baltimore*, which
    was published in 1906.

22   Tea Culture

The Experiment in South Caroina
BY DR. CHARLES U. SHEPARD, Special Agent in Charge of Tea Culture
    Investigations
Washington, D.C., 1899
    This is Report Number 61 of the U.S. Department of Agricul-
    ture. Tea was successfully grown in the lowcountry in the late
    nineteenth century but proved too expensive to harvest. Some of
    the bushes can still be seen around Summerville. This bulletin
    has nothing on drawing tea.

23 The Southern Cookbook

[Charleston, S.C.?] 1901

These were tested receipts compiled by the Woman's Department of the South Carolina Interstate and West Indian Exposition, December 1, 1901, to May 31, 1902.

24 The Carolina Rice Cook Book

Charleston, S.C., 1901

This was compiled by Mrs. Samuel G. Stoney and published by the Carolina Rice Association. She notes the names of friends and plantations with some of her recipes and credits various cooks without giving surnames or neighborhood, probably most of them on plantations. There is a lyrical page on cooking and eating rice birds. Fifty-odd of these recipes are from *The Carolina Housewife*.

25 The Spartanburg Dames' Recipe Book

Published under the Auspices of the Ladies' Kennedy Library Association
Spartanburg, S.C., 1902

Unless you count No. 4, this seems to have been the first up-country cookbook.

26 The Greenville Century Book

Comprising an Account of the First Settlement of the County and the Founding of the City of Greenville, S. C.
Greenville, S.C., 1903

Recipes and advertisements are found on pages 76–162.

27 Milady's Own Book

Charleston, S.C., 1905

Issued by the Fort Sumter Chapter of the South Carolina Division of Children of the Confederacy.

28   The Every Day Cook Book

Compiled by the ladies of the Village Improvement Society of Fort Mill,
  South Carolina
Charlotte, N.C., 1906

29   Culinary Crinkles Cook Book

As Gathered by the Senior Miriams of the Presbyterian Church of Green-
  wood, S. C.
Greenwood, S.C., 1908
  Despite the dated title, the ladies of the First Presbyterian Church
  of Greenwood are to be complimented for their conscientious
  periodic revisions of this book. *See* No. 40.

30   Charleston Receipts

COMPILED BY E. L. K.
Decorated by Fanny Mahon King
[Charleston, S.C.? 1910?]
  No place or date are given.

31   Tested Recipes of Practical People

Ladies Aid Society, Congregation Sinai
Sumter, S.C., 1910
  This is the first of several cookbooks put out by women's orga-
  nizations within Jewish congregations. Some of them are not
  kosher but at least one is.

32   Cookery Text Book

Greenville, S.C., 1910
  This was the work of Clara H. Graves, director of domestic
  science in the Young Women's Christian Association of Mon-
  aghan Mills, Greenville.

33   The Chester Cook Book

Edited by the Ladies' Aid—Baptist Church
Yorkville, S. C., 1910
> This originated from the Baptist Church of Chester. Someone
> deserves praise for the apostrophe in "Ladies' Aid."

34   Suggestions for Charleston Tea

Charleston, S.C., 1910
> This was published for the benefit of the King's Daughters
> Nursery.

35   Among the Pots and Pans

Published by the Pee Dee Chapter, Daughters of the American Revolution,
*   Bennettsville, S. C.*
Yorkville, S.C., 1911

36   Milady's-Own-Book

Ladies Aid Society of Grace Episcopal Church, Camden, S. C.
Columbia, S.C., 1916
> Not to be confused with No. 27.

37   The Spartanburg Cook Book

Spartanburg, S.C., 1917
> This was the work of the Social Workers of the local Methodist
> Episcopal Church.

38   Fifty Valuable and Delicious Recipes Made With Corn Meal

BY CELESTINE EUSTIS
Aiken, S.C., 1917

39   Best War Recipes

Ladies' Aid Society, Presbyterian Church, Sumter, S. C.
[Columbia, S.C.?] 1917

40   Culinary Crinkles Cook Book

Revised by the Women of the Church
Greenwood, S.C., 1922
    This was the second edition of No. 29.

41   The Autobiography of a Chameleon

BY DAISY BREAUX
Washington, D.C., 1930
    "Diasy Breaux" was Cornelia Donovan O'Donovan Calhoun,
who includes reminiscences of the St. Cecilia Society and of
Charleston food.

42   200 Years of Charleston Cooking

*Recipes Gathered by Blanche S. Rhett and edited by Lettie Gay, with an
   Introduction and Explanatory Matter by Helen Woodward*
New York, N.Y., 1930
    This was reprinted twice, in 1930 and in 1931, and later reis-
sued by the University of South Carolina Press. First published
during Prohibition it contains amusingly coy references to alco-
holic beverages. *See also* No. 44.

43 The Loss of Iron, Copper, and Manganese in Cooking Vegetables by Different Methods

Submitted in Partial Fulfillment of the Requirement for the Degree of Master of Science in the Department of Chemistry of the University of South Carolina.

BY FRANCIS BARTOW CULP.

Columbia, S.C., 1933

Proved that steaming preserved the mineral content of vegetables better than other methods of cooking them. At this time nutritionists had become aware that vegetables grown in South Carolina had an unusually high iodine content and that insufficient iodine in the diet caused goiter. For a number of years the words "The Iodine State" were cast in South Carolina automobile license plates, to the puzzlement of all but nutritionists.

44 200 Years of Charleston Cooking

Recipes Gathered by Blanche S. Rhett and edited by Lettie Gay, with an Introduction and Explanatory Matter by Helen Woodward

New York, N.Y., 1934

A second edition of No. 42, slightly expanded and more complacent about alcohol. Apparently the revisions were precipitated by the repeal of Prohibition.

45 Feeding the Family

Health Cook Book

BY HELEN GERTRUDE RANDLE

Assisted by J. H. Tilden and William Gunter Davis

Greenville, S.C., 1934

NOTES

NOTES

NOTES

NOTES